In Season and Out, Homilies for Year C

In Season and Out, Homilies for Year C

William J Grimm

UCAN ⋅))》

2015

ISBN
9781925371000   Hardback
9781925371017   Paperback
9781925371024   ePub
9781925371031   Kindle
9781925371048   Pdf

Layout by UCAN and Astrid Sengkey
Cover design by Astrid Sengkey. Original artwork 'The Road to Emmaus' by He Qi.
© 2013. All rights reserved.
Text Minion Pro Size 10 &11

Published by:

An imprint of the ATF Ltd.
PO Box 504
Hindmarsh, SA 5007
ABN 90 116 359 963
www.atfpress.com
Making a lasting impact

Table of Contents

Lent

Easter Season

Foreword

The Catholic Church lives on two lungs—Word and Sacrament. They reach their clearest expression and celebration for the Church's life in the Eucharist—the "source and summit of the Church's life" as Vatican 2 puts it.

Father William J Grimm is a Maryknoll Missioner of 40 years experience in Asia—mostly Japan, but Hong Kong and Cambodia as well. In that time he has come to deepen his understanding of the distinctiveness of the message and person of Jesus Christ even in circumstances and among people that Jesus could never have known or imagined.

Every week for the Church's three year liturgical cycle, Fr. Grimm gives visitors to www.ucanews.com—UCAN—the benefit of his learning, prayer, wisdom and experience. Each week, his homilies for Sundays and special feasts are seen by some 3,000 visitors to the main UCAN site and with subtitles on UCAN's Vietnamese and Chinese sites.

We are delighted to offer the texts of these pastoral homilies.

Michael Kelly SJ
Publisher
www.ucanews.com

First Sunday of Advent (C)

If someone said to me, "nations will be in anguish" or, "people will be terrified to death at what is going to happen," how would I answer?

"So? What else is new?"

Nations are always anguished over something or other, usually with good reason. Peace and justice always seem to be one more negotiation, one more election, one more ceasefire away. When things are going well politically, some sort of natural disaster seems inevitable.

When it comes to people being terrified, we know that is a description of each of us at least sometimes. Children live in a world of giants who say and do inexplicable things. Young people fear rejection by their peers. Students worry about courses and their future. Adults worry about their work and their children. The elderly worry about their health, their past and their future.

Perhaps that is the reason people in every age think theirs is the one of which Jesus spoke. So, let's assume that the Lord is talking of our age and our lives. What then? There must be a better answer than fearful concentration upon an impending doom that never quite arrives, yet whose threat never quite disappears.

"When these things begin to happen, stand up straight and raise your heads." Is that the way to face the anxieties of my life? Stiff upper lip?

But, there is more to Jesus' answer than platitudes like "keep on keeping on." He says the reason we should not give up is that our "ransom is near at hand." We have all been in situations where we needed some sort of "ransom," some rescue.

However, we will not be able to see that our ransom is at hand unless we are prepared to receive it. Jesus warns us to "be on guard" and singles out indulgence, drunkenness and worldly cares as the dangers we must avoid. Why point to them in particular? Why doesn't he warn us about wrong ideas or inadequate faith?

The thread that unites those dangers is cowardice. When I choose them, I have decided to run away from tensions and troubles to embrace oblivion or to crowd them out of my life with frenzied activity. But, though I may try to avoid them or close my eyes to problems, they will not go away. Even if I spend a lifetime at it, I will not be able to avoid the inevitability of death.

In order to be ransomed by the Lord, I need courage to accept the pain, confusion and disaster in my life. Only then can the Lord rescue me. The reason is plain: the Cross is the ultimate pain of the world and the healing of that pain. God Incarnate tortured to death rescues us. Only when we are willing to stand by our own crosses, confident that the Lord is with us, can the healing ransom offered by Christ be ours. If I run from the pain, I run from the place where I can meet the healer.

Advent ("Coming") is our time of waiting for the Lord, the Lord who will come at the end of time, but who also comes to us whenever we are willing to stay at the Cross — whether his or our own. The Lord has acted, and will act in the midst of pain and confusion.

Can I believe that when troubles come the Lord comes as well? How can I deepen my faith in that coming? The Lord's answer is "Pray constantly." That does not mean spending all my time on my knees. It means being constantly aware, or at least constantly reminding myself that the Lord is really with me.

In Advent we nurture our awareness that the Lord really has come and really comes. One way to do that is by remembering. Let's spend this season remembering how he has come many times when we were afraid and confused, and how the Lord brought us through. The remembering will enable us to "stand secure before the Son of Man."

Second Sunday of Advent (C)

We know we will be taken to a world of adventure when a tale opens with words like "Once upon a time." They prepare us for marvels — for knights in armor, damsels in silks, fierce dragons, talking animals, magic potions, helpful elves, mischievous gnomes and mysterious fairies.

Compared with that, Luke's story of John is boring. How much adventure can we expect from a story that begins with names of rulers who mean little or nothing to us, detailed yet incomprehensible information about some date, and names of places that are hard to pronounce and that don't even exist any more?

Why couldn't the evangelist have just written, "Once upon a time in a land far, far away the word of God was spoken to John son of Zechariah in the desert."

The Bible does have "once upon a time" tales. The two creation accounts in Genesis, the Tower of Babel, Noah's Ark, Balaam's talking donkey, Jericho's walls falling to trumpet blasts — all are such tales. Like poetry or good fiction, they are true, but not factual. It is true that God created the world in power and love to be good. That is the truth of the creation stories, which are not factual at all.

Luke tells us that wonderful things are going to happen. "Every valley shall be filled and every mountain and hill shall be leveled. The windings shall be made straight and the rough ways smooth, and all flesh shall see the salvation of God."

That sounds like a "once upon a time" tale, and if it were a fairy tale, we would listen to it in a certain way.

However, Luke is not telling a fairy tale. His story is real, the most real story, the truest story that ever was. In this story, God's truth and the world's facts are not merely close, they are together in Jesus.

Therefore, we know that the way of the Lord will be prepared for real, and all shall see the salvation of God for real.

Reality — that is Luke's message. He tells of a reality that can be located in time and place. So, we get facts of geography, chronology and history. It is Luke's way of saying, "Hear this story as you hear no other. This story goes beyond what you think of as fact or truth."

That is an important message for us in Advent. This is the season in which we recommit ourselves to live in anticipation of the fulfillment of God's promises. It is a time to recall that those promises are real and that God intends them to be true in the real world, the world in which we live in flesh, not fantasy.

The vocation of John the Baptizer is the vocation of us Christians, the Church. He was a herald announcing the coming of God's Kingdom. So are we. He came in a particular time, "the fifteenth year of the rule of Tiberius Caesar," to a particular place, "the entire region of the Jordan."

Each of us lives in a particular time and in a particular place. And in that time and place, the word of God is spoken to each of us, giving us the vocation to call upon the world to "Make ready the way of the Lord."

We live in expectation of the coming of the Lord. That coming is not a once upon a time thing nor a someday, somewhere, somehow thing. The coming of God to me, the call of God to me, and my response to that call are something that happens today. It happens in a certain time and a certain place. It calls me to respond with my real life here and now.

Advent is the season in which the Church recommits itself to living a great adventure. We are a band of companions walking through a world of marvels and dangers to a promised goal, eternal life with God. The band is real, the world is real, the marvels are real, the dangers are real. The goal is real.

Third Sunday of Advent (C)

Among the popular features of many newspapers are advice columns. Readers send questions to the columnists, who then provide answers.

We like to get answers to our problems. If someone is able to suggest a quick fix to them, we are happy. It has always been that way, and probably always will.

Various people came to John the Baptizer in the desert to get advice. He gave it.

He told the crowd in general to share. He told tax collectors (a notoriously corrupt group in his time) to be honest. He told soldiers to not abuse their power by abusing people.

We are not told how they reacted to John's advice, but since group after group asked for it, we can assume that folks liked what he had to say. We can be less sure that they actually followed it. My own experience of giving and receiving advice makes me suspect that they did not.

Apparently, the people who heard John were looking for something other than advice. Otherwise, they would have followed it, and the world would be a different place. Equally apparent is the fact that I am not really looking for advice, though I may listen to talks, read books and scan articles which I then ignore. I have some other desire, a desire symbolized by my hopeful search for good advice.

What are we really looking for? Answers or an answer? Occasionally, we see signs or hear people who say, "Jesus is the Answer." The irreverent comeback is, of course, "What's the question?"

Well, what is the question? What am I looking for? What is the desire?

I think it is a special kind of relationship. Perhaps that is the real meaning of those "Jesus is the Answer" declarations. John offered advice. The One who came after, who was "mightier" than John, seldom offered advice. Frequently, we see him ignoring requests for advice. Instead, he invites people to a new kind of relationship with God and other people.

A common question at this time of year is, "What do you want for Christmas?" When I was a child, my father used to reply, "All I want is some well-behaved kids." We always found it easier to give him a necktie.

The Lord asks each of us the same question. "What do you want for Christmas?" His asking frees me from the necessity of thinking of one more thing that will clutter my life. I can turn to him and say, "Lord, all I want is to know you, to know how close to me you are, how much you love me."

It's a cliché in Advent and Christmas time to mouth wishes for world peace, but the Lord does not even offer that. What he offers is himself. If we really accept that gift, we will find peace.

The acceptance is the key. When John offered advice, people could accept it or reject it and carry on with their lives. If they accepted it, they became nicer people and the world became a nicer place. Nicer, that's all. It remained the same old world. If we become nicer, the world would still be the same old world.

The Lord comes to clear it all away. "His winnowing fan is in his hand to clear his threshing floor." The Lord offers something totally new, totally different. He offers a world where advice is not needed, where our baptism "in the Holy Spirit and in fire" will make of us a new creation.

What we really want has already been given us. We do not have to wait until Christmas Day to receive it. We do not have to wait until we start following all the good advice we have received.

We can spend our lives looking for John the Baptizer, looking for the right advice, the right rules, the right morality by which to live. Or, we can accept the Christmas gift offered us at every moment, the loving presence of Jesus Christ the Lord.

Fourth Sunday of Advent (C)

Sometimes, I meet someone and know the child he or she once was because the child has grown up, but has never been outgrown. There is a spontaneous friendliness, a wonder at life and grace that could only belong to that child.

On the other end of life, I look at an infant or child and wonder what sort of grandmother or grandfather I am seeing. Will this child grow in wisdom and grace and be a blessing to all? Will she live a full lifetime? Will he be marred terribly by the injustice, pain and suffering that are inevitable in any life? Will she be forced to endure more than a fair share of that injustice, pain and suffering? Will he cause joy or pain?

Luke's Gospel presents two pregnant women. Luke tells us that each had reason to believe the child she carried was a son. We are also told that each of them was pregnant through an extraordinary act of God. Otherwise, they knew as little as any mother does about the child she bears. What their children would become was as much a mystery to Mary and Elizabeth as any child is a mystery to us.

Elizabeth's child became a desert-dwelling religious teacher who taught his disciples how to live before God. His forthright fulminations against evil eventually cost him his life.

Mary's child followed his father's trade as a carpenter. Later, he became an itinerant preacher. Eventually, he, too, paid with his life for what he became.

What would Mary and Elizabeth have done if they had known in advance the lives their sons would live? Would they have despaired? Would they have terminated their pregnancies? Would they have done all in their power to prevent their sons' choosing the paths they eventually traveled? We don't know.

We are about to celebrate the birth of Jesus. We see pictures and statuettes of the child in the manger. We watch movies and television programs about children and "the spirit of Christmas." In many places, Christmas has become a festival for children.

Christmas is, of course, much more than a child's feast. But, it is, indeed, a time for us to reflect upon children and the gifts we give them, the legacy we leave them. It is not always a good one.

One of the dispiriting things at this time of year is adults' supporting unbridled selfishness in children. For many, Christmas is the season of "Give me." But, the point of gifting is the giving, not the receiving. I knew a child who at Christmas time would go with her parents to an orphanage to share her parents with children who had none.

There is much that we do throughout the year to our children that warps the promise with which they are born. We provide them with "entertainment" that is, in effect, a form of child abuse, because it will malform the child that God has given to the world as a unique gift. We may bring the child to church and provide for some religious education, but then show that our day-to-day lives bear no relation to the Gospel we claim should be the guiding principle of our lives.

A speaker once asked her audience, "If you die tonight, will your children go to heaven?" That simple question contains the challenge and the glory of a parent's vocation. But, it is not limited to parents. We all play a part in raising the children of the world. Are we giving them all they need to be children of God through all eternity?

Mary and Elizabeth could not protect their children from the dangers of life. They could, however, raise their sons to be men for whom faithfulness to God was more important than life itself.

Can we do the same for our children? We will not be able to protect them from life, but we can point out to them the road to heaven. We can take them with us as we journey along that road. Can there be a better Christmas gift than that?

Holy Family (C)

What sort of parents could mislay their child for three days? And, what about the teachers in the temple? Didn't they ask Jesus where he was staying, where his parents were? Were they stupid? Did he lie to them?

Is the account of the boy Jesus in the temple about careless adults and a footloose though precocious 12-year-old? No, it is about the man he grew up to be.

The hint comes from the fact that it was on the "third day" that his parents found Jesus. For any Christian, that phrase brings to mind the Resurrection.

Luke presents this story not to tell us about the childhood of Jesus, but to give a synopsis of his Gospel, a summary that begins with the birth of John and ends with the discovery on the third day of Jesus who had been lost.

The synopsis presented as the infancy and childhood of Jesus is followed immediately by a shift to the future, to the prophetic ministry of John. It then moves through the activity of Jesus to his death and the disciples' encounter on the third day with the Risen One everyone thought was lost forever in death.

What can we learn about the life and mission of Jesus from the part of the summary that we hear today? It might be helpful to turn off our imagination for a few minutes, to drive from our minds the pictures we've seen of a boy sitting with bearded old men, looked at by a surprised lady in blue and a bearded man with a staff in his hand. Let's just look at the words of the account and see what they remind us of in the life of Jesus.

Luke's story takes place in Jerusalem at Passover, the feast of the liberation of the Hebrew people by an extraordinary work of God, the Exodus. Years later, at another Passover in Jerusalem, God freed all people from the power of sin and death through another extraordinary work, the Passion, Death and Resurrection of Jesus.

At the end of the celebration, the parents of Jesus think he is lost, though he is exactly where he belongs. After that Passover years later, the Emmaus story puts a pair of disciples on the road, thinking that Jesus is lost though he is exactly where he belongs — with them.

Then, Luke tells of finding of the child in the temple on the third day. The temple is the place of God in the world, the chief point of worship, the place where people could expect to experience the holiness of God. Jesus is there, because Jesus has become the new temple. (Remember that Luke tells us the old temple's veil was torn apart when Jesus died).

In the temple, Jesus is among the teachers, because he is a teacher. Luke intends to share Jesus's teaching, so from the start he is among the teachers. However, Jesus is much more than a teacher. He is the Son of God. Therefore, he says, "Did you not know I had to be in my Father's house?"

The mystification of his parents, who "did not grasp what he said to them" is paralleled by people in every age who are mystified by Jesus. However, mystification does not mean separation. Jesus stayed with his parents as he stays with his Church. As the boy Jesus "increased in wisdom and in years and in divine and human favor," so, too, the Church grows in wisdom, years and favor.

This Gospel story, then, is not a story about the child Jesus. It is a story of the Gospel as Luke plans to present it to us. In this liturgical year, we will reflect upon that Gospel of Luke. We will re-affirm our commitment to follow the teachings of Jesus, to recognize him as the true Son of God, the temple where God dwells among us. We will struggle as a community of faith and as individuals to grow in wisdom and favor with God and the world.

Epiphany (C)

Scholars tell us the earliest feasts of the Church were Easter, Pentecost and Epiphany. The Annunciation (original feast of the Incarnation), Christmas and all the others came later.

Originally, Epiphany celebrated several events in the life of Christ, including his birth, the adoration of the magi, the hidden years of Jesus' youth, his baptism by John and his first miracle at the wedding in Cana. What all those events have in common is that they were "introductions" of Jesus to the world.

In the Western Church, Epiphany eventually developed into three feasts: Christmas, the Epiphany feast as we celebrate it today and the Baptism of the Lord. Each of them commemorates and celebrates some aspect of the manifestation or appearing of the Lord, his introduction to the world.

While there is something to be said for the later development of three feasts from one, let's look at them together, seeing what unified message they might have for us today.

First, the Christmas aspect, the manifestation of Jesus as one of us. We can get so caught up with Mary and Joseph, the baby, the manger, the angels, the shepherds, the wise men and so on, that we can forget that the feast is not about birth so much as about a manifestation, the showing of God as one of us, born to live, grow, learn, love, die and rise.

Think about that. If we want to see God, we need not spend years doing spiritual calisthenics or wait until we die. God has come among us as one of us. If you wish to see God, look at Jesus, the manifestation of God among us.

And not simply among us. The second aspect of this feast is the fact that Jesus is one of us for us. The wise men from the east who come to adore Jesus symbolize the wise men and women of all times and places who are invited to come to Jesus. In welcoming those worshipers from pagan lands, Christ shows that his coming is not limited to a particular time or place or even religion. He is here for us all, and the salvation he brings is meant for all, including even those who do not know him.

The third aspect of the original Epiphany feast now celebrated separately is the Baptism of the Lord, next Sunday's feast. When the Father proclaims, "This is my beloved son," it is obviously a manifestation of Jesus as the Christ, the Messiah.

But, there is more to the Lord's baptism than that proclamation. His baptism marks the end of his "hidden years" and the beginning of Jesus' public ministry. The Lord is among us and for us with a purpose.

That purpose is the proclamation to all the world of the love of God. That love is the reason for the Incarnation and Jesus shows that love to us in his teaching, his healing and above all in his cross.

In our own baptism, we are united with Christ. So, what we say about him is, in some way, something we say about ourselves. What does looking at the three aspects of Epiphany teach us about our own vocation as Christians?

The Christmas aspect certainly applies to me. After all, I am a born-and-bred human being, as was Jesus. But, it's not so simple as that. I too often try to avoid the implications of being human. I pile up goods, run after fads, and give myself over to idols of wealth, status, nation, culture and even religion to hide from myself the fact that I am weak, mortal. I allow myself to forget that real human life is lived in community with others, a community of shared love and concern. Like Jesus, I must manifest the presence of God who is love.

And my showing that love of God must not be limited. It is easy to love those whom I like, those similar to myself. But the wise men were not like Jesus. They were foreigners. They were pagans. Our own community must be as open to the world, accepting those children of our Father who are different from us, whether in race, nation, gender, sexuality, religion, politics or physical or mental abilities and disabilities.

Finally, we must, like Jesus, accept that vocation to manifest God to the world. We must make that a part of our lives, shaping who we are and what we do. When we do that, we become an epiphany, an introduction of God and the world.

Baptism of the Lord
First Sunday of the Year (C)

People who went to be baptized by John were looking for a Messiah, an anointed one who would fulfill their deepest needs and hopes.

What were those needs and hopes that brought them to the desert? For some, they took a political form, release from the Roman Empire's taxation and oppression. Others wanted to see the unambiguous presence of God among the chosen people.

For still others, it was probably vaguer and, therefore, perhaps deeper. They sought some sort of inner peace. They hoped someone could give them a good reason to risk getting out of bed in the morning and take the bigger risk of closing their eyes at night. They wanted some sign that their lives were noticed by God, important to God, embraced by God and sustained forever by God. In other words, those folks at the side of the Jordan were like us.

Among those folks was Jesus. He, too, had come to John. He, too, received John's baptism. Perhaps he, too, was looking for something, some assurance of his relationship with God. In other words, Jesus at the side of the Jordan was like us.

"When all the people were baptized, and Jesus was at prayer after likewise being baptized, the skies opened and the Holy Spirit descended on him in visible form like a dove. A voice from heaven was heard to say, 'You are my beloved Son. On you my favor rests.'"

In that moment, Jesus received the assurance he was waiting for, the answer to his heart's desire. So, too, did everyone else. That is the reason for the Spirit's appearance in visible form. The assurance to Jesus that he had God's favor was also an assurance to the rest of the crowd that in Jesus, God's favor was on them, too. It is our assurance as well.

The difference between us Christians and the rest of the world is the knowledge that there is an answer for our anticipating hearts, and the answer is the Son of God present among us. That was Good News to the people on the banks of the Jordan River. It is Good News for the whole world.

The celebration of the baptism of Jesus is a proclamation of who he is, the first public proclamation of the identity of Jesus, the Son of God. The Holy Spirit tells those who have been full of anticipation that their hopes are realized.

In fact, their hopes have been exceeded. They were willing to settle for John as their messiah. John, however, told them that the real messiah would be vastly more powerful than himself.

What they — and we — were given is the Son of God. Sometimes we take that for granted. We treat the title as if it were an interesting batch of words. Perhaps the marvel of what the words mean is too great for us to grasp them even slightly, so we shrug them off.

However, the voice at the Baptism of Jesus was telling the truth. God has given us not only the answer to our hearts' anticipation; God has given us the fullness of God-ness to be with us, to stay with us.

So what are we to do? Should we sit back and luxuriate? The answer to our hearts' desires does not entail resting or relaxing. It doesn't even bring much comfort. It brings something else, something that is a theme of the Gospel of Luke that we reflect upon this year. It brings a call to spread the Good News, to share it with the whole world.

The same thing happened with Jesus. After receiving the Baptism of John and the declaration of his identity, he headed off deeper into the wilderness to be tempted, and then began his mission.

We, too, have been baptized — in our case, with the Baptism of Jesus. We, too, face temptations. We, too, are given a mission as a result of our Baptism and the declaration that Jesus is the Son of God.

We are sent into the world to be advertisements in our words and deeds for the answer to the heart's anticipation of the world, the Son of God, Jesus Christ.

Second Sunday of the Year (C)

John's Gospel tells us that Mary was at a wedding party. Then, it mentions that Jesus and his disciples "had likewise been invited." It sounds as if their invitation had been tacked onto Mary's.

Why would someone have asked her to bring them along? I can't imagine any other reason than that Jesus and his disciples were the kind of folks you want at a wedding party. They must have been witty, good singers and dancers and a good audience for other people's jokes. We seldom think of Jesus and his disciples in that way, but there are plenty of reasons why we should.

The story of the wedding feast at Cana actually focuses upon a joke, a pun by Jesus. Unfortunately, like all word plays, the puns of Jesus get lost in translation, so unless we learn Aramaic (with a Galilean drawl besides), we miss the joke. Anyway, Jesus joked with his mother.

Mary said to him, "They have no wine." Had she said it in English, Jesus might have responded, "Of course not, it's a happy day. Why should anyone whine?" Mary then would have made a face, groaned and pretended to ignore the pun.

Well, that is what happened. Of course, Jesus and Mary did not speak English. But, in the Galilean dialect of Aramaic (a dialect ridiculed by the sophisticates in Jerusalem because of its sloppy pronunciation), it was possible to make a pun connecting "wine" and "lamb." Jesus did so, acting as if Mary had said, "They have no lamb."

This makes sense, then, of the answer Jesus gave Mary: "My hour has not yet come." Just before the account of the wedding feast the evangelist tells us how John the Baptizer had pointed to Jesus and said, "Look, there is the Lamb of God!" Mary talked of wine, but Jesus affirmed John's declaration, adding that the time had not yet come for him to show himself as the Lamb of God.

Like many mothers who've spent years listening to their children's jokes, Mary made a face and ignored her son's pun. Instead, she in effect told him to get down to business and do what the Lamb should do. And he did it.

He gave wine. Jesus knew the difference between a good and a mediocre wine. According to the waiter in charge, he gave good wine. There were good reasons for his doing that. The most obvious is that he drank wine and knew how enjoyable a really good wine can be. The second reason is linked to who he is.

In Scripture, wine is a symbol of joy and peace. The joy is easy to understand, but how is wine a symbol of peace? There is more to drinking wine than uncorking a bottle. The wine has to be made. That requires vineyards. They require lots of care. Then, the grapes must be harvested. Finally, the wine must be made. If soldiers or marauders destroy the vineyard or drive off the workers, there will be no wine. If we have wine, that means we have peace.

Jesus makes wine. That is, he brings a time of peace to the world. We live in that time.

We do? The world certainly does not look peaceful. Even the Church is not peaceful. And, while we're at it, neither am I. What is this peace that Jesus is giving when he turns mere everyday water into wine?

We must return to his pun. The wine he gives is himself, the Lamb of God who takes away the sin of the world. The real lack of peace in the world and in my life is not something political or psychological. The real lack of peace, and the cause of all other lack of peace, is spiritual. It is enslavement to sin.

Jesus the Lamb presents us with the wine of peace because he overcomes the sin of the world in his death and resurrection.

What remains for us is the task of the head waiter, the one who recognized the good wine and served it to the guests. If, through prayer, refection and service, I imbibe the Good News and, intoxicated by it, go out to the world filled with the Spirit of Christ, I and the world will know peace.

Third Sunday of the Year (C)

The Bible is reputedly the best-selling book in history. There is, however, no evidence that it is the best-read book.

In the past century, Biblical scholarship has made great progress in providing tools to gain a deeper understanding of Scripture than has been possible for centuries. That scholarship has borne fruit in translations, courses, books, pamphlets and programs aimed at drawing us to a new encounter with the Word of God. Have they done so?

Unfortunately, they have not succeeded. Too few people nourish their faith at the banquet of the Word. Of those who turn to Scripture, too many do so in a fundamentalist way that ignores the tools of scholarship and the guidance of the Church.

Why should we be more familiar with the Bible? Isn't it enough that on Sunday morning we hear three passages and a psalm read (or, if we are lucky, proclaimed) in church? Why should we spend extra time reading and studying a book written long, long ago in strange times and tongues?

One reason is that it is our book. I was once in an ecumenical group where the leader held up a Bible and asked, "Whose book is this?" The Protestant members present each answered, "It's God's." Then, the leader turned to me and said, "I hope you get this one right, because I want you to give us the Catholic position. Whose book is this?" I answered, "The Church's." The leader was satisfied.

For a Catholic, one who sees the Bible as first and foremost the Church's treasure, that book belongs to us as intimately as anything can. It is we, the Church, who in response to God's action among us wrote it, or, in the case of the Old Testament, made it our own. It is we, the Church, that handed it on from generation to generation. It is we, the Church, that have striven to make it come alive in every age in the lives of Christians.

The Word of God is, or should be, a reminder of God's presence among us. That is the reason we treat a Bible or Lectionary with special respect. It is the reason liturgists cringe when they see the Word being proclaimed from a leaflet or photocopy.

When Ezra read the book of God's Word to the people they also listened to his explanation. Ezra spoke to the community on behalf of the community. He was its own voice, commissioned to explain the community's understanding of the Word of God.

The Church, too, has explained the Scriptures over the centuries. Those explanations take various forms: doctrinal teachings, homilies, classes, scholarship and Scripture sharing in small groups. The important point is that we try to read and hear the Word of God as the Church's word and reflect upon it guided by that community.

In the opening of his Gospel, Luke gives a simple description of what Scripture is, "a narrative of the events which have been fulfilled in our midst." God's relationship with us is not a matter of words or a book. God relates through deeds, "events." Scripture provides a narrative of those events and of the community's response to them. It also provides a model of how to view God's action in our own lives. Scripture is a "lens" through which we look for, find and understand God at work in the world.

Jesus in the synagogue shows us how it is done. Isaiah had written about a time when God's promise would be fulfilled, "a year of favor from the Lord." It would be a time of liberty and healing. The passage describes that time as one of comfort, joy and justice. Luke does not show Jesus reading the whole passage because people were familiar enough with Scripture that hearing the opening would bring the entire passage to mind, but Jesus is certainly referring to the entire section.

He is using the Word of God to announce to the people of Nazareth that the time had come for the fulfillment of God's promises. The new age has dawned. Folks in the synagogue understood that and its implications because they knew the Scriptures. We live in that new age. If we wish to understand what that means for us and the world, let's start by deepening our knowledge of and love for the Word of God.

Fourth Sunday of the Year (C)

Folks in Nazareth knew Jesus well. He had grown up in their village. They knew his family. Probably some of them were relatives. They were a bit mystified at his wisdom. After all, "Isn't this Joseph's son?" Perhaps that was the problem.

Folks in Nazareth had their own ideas of a savior, whether or not they talked about them or even brought them to their own minds. What did they get, though? "Joseph's son." How prosaic! Could they really be expected to accept as their savior someone they had known since he was a kid?

On top of that, he told them they should not expect him to work wonders for them, even though he knew they wanted them. "You will doubtless quote me the proverb, 'Physician, heal yourself,' and say 'Do here in your own country the things we have heard you have done in Capernaum.'"

All in all, Jesus is a disappointing savior. He certainly does not fulfill the job description the folks in Nazareth would set for him. He does not fulfill mine either. Jesus is an underachiever.

Either there is something wrong with Jesus, or there is something wrong with our expectations. We either have to abandon him as a savior or accept him on his own terms. There seems to be no other possibility.

That is probably why so many do not bother with him. It is also the reason that many of us who claim to be his followers actually do not follow him. We give him lip-service, but in fact do not live as if we really thought of Jesus as our savior. Sometimes we reinvent him, deciding to believe in someone whom we call "Jesus Christ," but who bears only passing resemblance to Christ himself.

The problem with Jesus is that he is not extraordinary enough for us. He really is "Joseph's son." He really is someone from a small town in northern Israel. We want special effects and we get a carpenter's son. Why don't we like that?

If the savior of the world is to be found talking in his hometown synagogue to the people among whom he grew up, then we must face the fact that salvation does not occur in some sort of special state where everything is wonderful. Salvation happens in our own villages, whether they be small towns like Nazareth or the global village.

We don't want that because, as often as not, we think salvation should rescue us from our humdrum or painful lives. We don't want our everyday homes, our everyday work, our everyday lives to be the place where God saves. However, our savior does not save us from our lives, but in our lives. Like it or not, our lives are sacred.

What can we do about that? Well, presuming that we agree to accept Jesus on his terms, we will have to do something about the way we live. That means looking for God's work of salvation in day-to-day prosaic events, the joys and pains of our lives.

How can we do that? The first step is to remind ourselves often throughout the day that the Lord is with us, is loving us. Morning prayers, prayers before meals, a quick prayer before doing something, night prayers — all these are helps. Then, perhaps all we need do is wait and see what happens.

Had the folks in Nazareth waited and paid more attention to Joseph's son instead of expelling him from the town, just think of the surprises that would have been in store for them.

Fifth Sunday of the Year (C)

Feeling unworthy of God's call is nothing new. Isaiah had the same problem: "Woe is me, I am doomed! For I am a man of unclean lips, living among a people of unclean lips." Peter says, "Leave me, Lord. I am a sinful man."

God, however, seems to be less demanding of us than we are ourselves. God will accept or, rather, work with and through our weaknesses.

In Isaiah's case his unclean lips were burned clean by a seraph-borne ember. Peter got words: "Do not be afraid. From now on you will be catching people."

Their reactions are important. The first words that pass Isaiah's newly-purified lips are, "Here I am; send me." Peter does not say anything; he acts. He and his partners "brought their boats to land, left everything, and became his followers."

"Vocation" comes from a word meaning, "call." A vocation, though, is not simply a call, as if God were yodeling in the heavens. It is a call to do something. Usually, we use the words "calling" or "vocation" about some work that involves one's whole being in service.

What are Isaiah and Peter called to do? Isaiah hears the voice of God saying, "Whom shall I send? Who will go for us?" Peter is told that he will become a fisher of people.

Apparently, the call is not so much to be something as to do something. A vocation is not to some special state of goodness. Even less is it a call to a special status. It is a call to a special task.

The error of Isaiah and Peter was that they thought they had to be a special kind of person to respond to God's call. They thought that the sort of persons they were, rather than the task to which they were called, should determine God's work in the world.

God's answer is simply, "Yes, I know you're not perfect. I'm not interested in that. I'm interested in having word of my love shared with the world. In a world where everyone is my specially loved child and everyone is imperfect, I am calling you to do something special for me. I don't need someone who can earn my love by being perfect. I just need you."

Catholics tend to identify the word "vocation" with a particular kind of response to God's call: priesthood or Religious life. However, they are not really vocations. They are ways of living the vocation each Christian has. Each of us Christians is called like Isaiah, like Peter, to do something for God. Just like Isaiah and Peter, we are called to proclaim God's message to the world, to be fishers of people, drawing them into deeper communion with God.

Like Isaiah and Peter, we have responded. In our Baptism, we have said, "Here I am; send me." In our Baptism, we have left our old life behind to follow Jesus. Baptism is an answer to a call, even though we might not fully realize it at the time.

So, to be Christian is to have a vocation. We are not perfect. Like Peter, I am sinful. Like Isaiah, I live among an unclean people. That is not important.

What is important is that God has called me. I am unworthy. I know that. God knows that. The people to whom God wants me to go either know that already or will know it soon enough.

It's not a matter of worthiness. It's a matter of the call. We should not get the two mixed up. My sinfulness is, in a sense, irrelevant. What counts is the task to which I have been called as an individual and to which we have been called as a Church.

The world is starving to hear of God's love, to see God's love. The world is swimming around in confusion, waiting to be brought into God's net. That is what counts. That is the vocation you and I have as Christians. God is willing to work with sinners like Isaiah, Peter, you and me. Let's give thanks for that and get to work.

Sixth Sunday of the Year (C)

When the British army surrendered, ending the American War of Independence, the English military band played a tune called "The World Turned Upside Down." The lyrics talk of cats chasing dogs, cheese eating mice and fish swimming in the air. When it comes to the world being turned upside down, however, the song cannot match what Jesus says.

The poor have everything. The hungry are full. The sad are happy. The insulted are blessed. The rich are losers. The full are hungry. The happy are pitiable. The popular are doomed. That certainly sounds like the world turned upside down.

Or, does it? Does Jesus really turn the world upside down? Perhaps the world is upside down to begin with, and therefore we cannot recognize it when it is set right. Maybe Jesus is calling us to be right side up.

That's hard to believe. I've known rich people and I've known poor people. The poor do not seem happier than the rich, nor do the rich seem miserable. Hungry people are really hungry, and when I finish a big meal, I don't feel empty. Happy people really do seem happy. Suffering people really are miserable. And, people who are liked really seem happier and healthier than those who are unpopular.

All of that is so obvious that we base our lives on those facts. We live in the real world, and that world has rules for getting along. If we follow them, we may be successful. If we don't follow them, we will almost certainly not be "healthy, wealthy and wise."

But, what if what we think of as the "real world" were not real after all? What if the things we have to do to live effectively were as ridiculous as bouncing around on our heads from place to place? Should we pick ourselves up by the toes and begin to go around looking upside down? On what basis could we make such a radical decision?

The only reason we have for thinking that the world might be upside down is Jesus's say-so. Should we take his word for it? That depends upon who he is. If he be one among many moral or religious teachers, then the risk that instead of merely appearing to be upside down we might really turn ourselves upside down is great. Maybe he had a vision problem that I would buy into without evidence or good reason.

On the other hand, if Jesus be indeed who the Church has proclaimed him to be, then we had better take his word for the way the world is supposed to stand. After all, if anyone knows which end is up, it should be he.

I recite a creed that proclaims Jesus to be "true God of true God." But, if I really believed what I say, wouldn't I be turning my world, or letting him turn my world, upside down?

If today two billion Christians were, for the sake of our brothers and sisters, to stop looking for material comfort, what would happen to the world? There might be economic chaos. There might also be an end to hunger and injustice. The world would be turned upside down.

If today two billion Christians were, for the sake of serving others, to stop looking for our own pleasure, what would happen to the world? The "entertainment" industry might collapse. There might also be a healthy sharing of friendship, fellowship and joy. The world would be turned upside down.

If today two billion Christians were, for the sake of standing upright before God, to give up doing what makes us fit in and be popular in our twisted societies, what would happen to the world? We might be called fools and might even be persecuted or crucified. We might also be the light of the world. The world would be turned upside down.

The Gospel presents us with a decision and a consequence. We must decide who Jesus is, and upon what authority he says some very strange things. If we decide that he knows how the world is meant to function because he made it, then we have to accept the consequence. We have been living upside down.

In that case, we have to get right side up. It will look upside down. It will, after a lifetime the other way around, feel upside down. But, for the first time, we may see the world the way it looks to God.

Seventh Sunday of the Year (C)

The problem with having a verb "to love" is that we can think of loving as a thing that concerns primarily ourselves. If I say, "I love," then I am the subject of the sentence. It can easily become a matter of me and my feelings. So long as my feelings are "warm and fuzzy," then I can consider myself a lover.

In Japanese, one does not "love," one *does* love." The verb is "do." That means that the focus is not on my emotional state, but my actions.

Today's Gospel passage says much the same thing. Everyone knows that Jesus told us to love. We are to love God and our neighbor. Does that mean that we are to cultivate warm feelings about them?

Apparently not. The only reference Jesus makes to feelings is, "Do to others what you would have them do to you" — figure out what you like, what makes you feel good, and then do it for someone else.

Unfortunately, that's not all that Jesus says. He doesn't tell me to find people I like and then do nice things for them. The entire list of people he says we should do love toward are the sort of people with whom I'd rather have nothing at all to do: people who hate me, people who abuse me, people who steal from me, strangers who beg from me — all sorts of unsavory folk.

It's not that I hate such people. I just want to live far away from them. But Jesus tells me that though I do not have to work up warm feelings toward their ilk, I have to overcome my cold feelings enough to serve them.

So, must I grit my teeth and inflict my goodness on those people? Saint Paul, who had a good memory for injuries, quotes Proverbs approvingly: "If your enemies are hungry, feed them; if they are thirsty, give them something to drink; for by this you will heap burning coals on their heads." Be nice to them so as to embarrass them? This is not Paul at his best.

No, the model has to be Jesus on the Cross, not only forgiving his murderers, but making excuses for them. "They don't know what they are doing."

Can we actually do that? Isn't it impossible to do love for all those people I'd rather avoid? Perhaps I could just have good feelings for them from afar.

But, the Lord will not allow that. I will have to eventually take a deep breath and plunge into actually meeting and serving those very people.

How can I do it? I wish I didn't know, but I do. In fact, I am experienced at it.

There are many people who have harmed me. There are people who have deprived me of what is rightfully mine. There are people who have made a fool of me. In most cases, I avoid them. There is one such person, however, that I cannot avoid.

My worst enemy is myself. The one who keeps me from living the life God calls me to is none other than myself. And yet, in spite of all I've done to myself over the years, I still feed myself, clothe myself, and, in general, look after myself. Like Jesus on the Cross making excuses for his enemies, I even make excuses for myself.

So, it is not totally impossible for me to do love toward an enemy. I just have to do for others what I do for myself. I have to be as willing to love the one I cross the street to avoid as I am to love the one I see in the mirror. That still is not easy. But, knowing I can do it for my worst enemy is an encouragement that I can do it for others.

There are other examples available to me. There are people who do love toward me, though I have harmed them either intentionally or unknowingly. Then, of course, there is God.

I am in many ways an enemy of God. Yet, God does not give up on me. God nurtures me, encourages me and challenges me. In a word, God does love toward me.

So, in my own life I can see the love of which Jesus speaks being done. I love myself, others love me, and God loves me.

That's a good head start. All I have to do is stretch myself a bit to do likewise for others.

Eighth Sunday of the Year (C)

Matthew's Gospel uses images of blind guides and planks in the eye to criticize Israel's religious leaders.

Religious leaders, whether shamans, imams, lamas, rabbis, ministers, or priests appear to be an integral part of being human. Thirty-five-thousand-year-old cave paintings show what appear to be shamans and some burials from that time appear to be their graves. While some Christian communities dispense with an official clergy, most recognize certain men and women as having a special role in the community.

People have high expectations of these leaders. They are often held to a different standard of behavior and are treated in special ways. Frequently, people even view religious leaders as having access to God that other people lack. That may be why people ask priests and ministers us to pray for them, yet one seldom hears clergy make requests to the laity for prayers.

Yet, they need those prayers. They are, indeed, guides for others, but even the best of them are sometimes blind guides. Even the best of them can be unaware of the planks in their own eyes. Generally, those weaknesses become a problem when they forget that their actions must be the verification of their teaching.

But, why do I digress into Matthew's message when today's passage is from Luke's Gospel? Matthew probably puts the words of Jesus in their original context, criticism of the religious leaders of Israel. However, Luke makes a very important change that may be easy to overlook. In Luke, Jesus warns all of his followers, whether we be leaders or not.

Why did Luke feel it necessary to redirect the message of Jesus from the Jewish leaders to the Christian faithful? Luke is very concerned with the mission of the Church. That mission is too important to be left to those who are guides and leaders within the Christian community. Every Christian is responsible.

Therefore, each Christian is a leader and guide for the world. The leadership of some within the Church is primarily aimed at assisting the leadership of all outside the Church.

A Japanese poem says: "Those who speak are noble; those who without knowing it themselves speak with their bodies are nobler. Those who give guidance are noble; those who without knowing it guide by example are nobler."

Actions do, indeed, speak louder than words. The people of the world are not looking for more words from the Church. People want to see the fruits of belief in action. They will find talk of God's love unbelievable if they do not first see that love.

That is the way we are to fulfill our mission as guides and teachers to the world. Luke rightfully takes what Jesus said of the leaders of his day and applies it to all of us.

We will know we are doing the right thing if we look to the fruits of our actions. As Jesus says today, "each tree is known by its yield." If through my life others have come to understand even a bit of the love and forgiveness of God, then I am a good tree.

Becoming a bearer of good fruit means that I must make the kind of self-examination that Jesus calls for. Do I really know where I am going in life or am I blind? Do I keep in view the object of my life journey, God? Do I pay attention to what God has taught through the Church and my own experience? Is my vision plank-blurred by sin, selfishness and laziness? Does my own life bear the fruit of a faithful life? Does my heart have an abundance from which I may speak and act?

Repentance, prayer, reflection and study will remove the obstacles that keep me from being a wise guide and a clear-visioned healer for the wandering children of God looking (unaware, perhaps) for a vision of the love of God made real in their lives.

Ninth Sunday of the Year (C)

When the German poet Heine was on his deathbed, a priest told him that God would forgive him. Heine replied: "Of course God will forgive me; that's His job."

I may not be so cynical as Heine, but in fact I do act as if I have hired God to take care of my spiritual problems just as I hire a plumber to take care of my piping problems or a dentist to see to my teeth. (Actually, considering that plumbers and dentists work in tight, damp, smelly places to seal up holes, they have a lot in common.) Anyway, I feel that God should put up with my failures, should take away all the unpleasantness in my life and not interfere with what I want to do. In return, I will give lip service — generally, if not exclusively, on Sundays and holy days.

But, God is not my employee. The simplest of all facts, yet the hardest to keep in mind, is that God is God and I am a creature. That gives me as much right to presume upon God as a centurion's soldiers or slaves had to presume upon him. None at all.

I should remember that and be amazed by the fact that after I say "Lord, I am not worthy" I am allowed to receive the Eucharist anyway. I am a sinner. My faith is weak. My deeds are seldom shaped by a desire to follow the will of God. Yet I receive the Body and Blood of Christ.

Obviously, God's care for me does not depend upon me. God loves me, not because it is the divine job description, but because God chooses to love me. And you. And even *them* (whoever they may be in your opinion). All unworthy. All loved.

That does not mean that we need not try to be pleasing to God. We should be anxious to return God's love by striving to be what we have been created to be, the children of God.

When the centurion admitted he was not worthy to have Jesus do anything for him, yet humbly hoped that Jesus would heal the slave, he showed the kind of relationship we must have with God.

The centurion's admission of unworthiness was acceptance of his humanity; his hope was an acknowledgment of God. He thus affirmed that God is God and that we are creatures, that simplest of facts that is the basis of faith. In response to that faith, a healing miracle occurred.

It was not the slave who asked Jesus for healing. He was incapable of going to Jesus himself, and as a slave he could not order anyone else to go on his behalf. It was the faith, prayer and action of one who loved him that brought about his healing.

There are many people who cannot go to God with their hopes and fears. Perhaps they do not believe. Perhaps they have despaired. Perhaps they don't want to bother God with their concerns. Perhaps they feel that their unworthiness makes them unlovable. Prayer is an unexplainable mystery, but we can and should pray on behalf of others, just as the centurion prayed on behalf of the slave.

This gives encouragement to those who ask the prayers of others. God's love is not limited by our inability to make a direct approach. The humble acknowledgment that we are weak and need the help of God is sufficient. For that reason, we need not use special words or rituals, though they are available and useful if we need them.

That does not mean that my prayers will be answered in the way I desire. There were many sick people in Jesus' day. He did not heal them all, or even many of them. He healed enough to teach us that our concerns are not ignored by God. Apparently that is more important than that we be rescued from our pains, doubts and crises. I may not think so when I am in anguish, but I am not worthy to dispute with God, who has declared love for me. With that word, I shall be healed.

Tenth Sunday of the Year (C)

In a world where mothers bury their children, God has a lot of explaining to do. Unfortunately, we have no reason to expect the explanations in this life. We can only look at God the Son on the Cross and know that within the mystery of the Trinity there is a parent's love for a dead child.

So, what good to millions of suffering mothers and fathers throughout history are stories of Elijah and Jesus returning two dead children to their mothers? What of the rest? Or, as a bereaved parent would say, "What of *mine*?" Bringing children to life thousands of years ago was well and good, but what about today?

In Dostoyevsky's novel *The Brothers Karamazov*, the sceptic Ivan speaks to his religious brother Alyosha of the suffering of children and how heavenly peace is not worth the suffering of a single child or its mother. "And so I hasten to give back my entrance ticket, and if I am an honest man I am bound to give it back as soon as possible. And that I am doing. It's not God that I don't accept, Alyosha, only I most respectfully return him the ticket."

Ivan is willing to face the problem and act on his conclusions. That is one way to deal with the problem. It is admirable, even if inadequate.

Did Luke include the story of the widow's son in his Gospel in order to torture everyone who ever hoped that Jesus would interrupt a funeral to bring back a dead son or daughter, wife or husband, father or mother, sister or brother, friend or relative? Or, did the evangelist have something else in mind?

The key to understanding what Luke is telling us is in verse 13 of the passage: "When the Lord saw [the mother], he had compassion for her." Until this point, Luke has used the word "Lord" either to refer to God or as a form of address like the modern "sir." Here, for the first time, Luke uses the word that

Greek-speaking believers used of God in order to refer to who Jesus is.

For Luke, what happens at the town gate of Naim is the first full presentation of Jesus the Lord as God with us. Until now, Jesus has healed diseases and infirmities and forgiven sins. Now it is time to see who he really is, not just one more wonder worker, but the One who has power over death.

Why would the situation of the widow at her son's funeral mark this change? Why is it here that Luke tells us that Jesus is God?

The greatest of human pains calls forth the greatest of human declarations, that God has walked among us. That is the essence of the good news. This is a world of suffering and death, but it is also the world where God became one with us.

Jesus shows himself as Lord in the situation that calls for the greatest compassion, in the situation that most typifies humanity, grief in the face of death. He feels it as we feel it. He is not a remote deity who cannot know what we feel from the inside. He knows as we know.

But, if he knows the pain of bereavement, why does he not remove it from our lives? He did it for that widow, why not for me?

Faith does not answer all questions. Pain, suffering, confusion and death are facts of life. Every life. Jesus is the Lord of life, yet he, too, dies. So eventually did that young man from Naim, his mother and everyone else in the crowd. So will I. So will everyone I love.

Christianity does not avoid that difficult fact nor explain it away by talking of reincarnation or the unreality of our lives here. To be a Christian is to accept the terrible and fearsome reality of death. We wish it were otherwise, but it isn't. Jesus was not playacting in the garden when he sweated blood at the thought of his death.

Obviously, God does not allow us to avoid death. Instead, the knowledge of death is one of the chief ways God uses to speak to us of love and true life. The death of the young is extra shocking. Therefore, it is an extra-strong call to faith.

That faith is trust in Jesus, the Crucified Son of God, the Lord of life who does not prevent funerals, but makes them into entry rites to eternal life where death's power will be overcome for all.

Eleventh Sunday of the Year (C)

We might say a sinner is someone who does wrong and we might even give a list of sins. Frequently confessions are like that. "Laundry lists," some priests call them, lists of sins that need cleansing.

But, are those sins the whole story? Is my laundry list about dirty socks, or about dirt? Are sins my disease or are they merely the symptoms of something more basically wrong in my life? Sneezing, coughing and a fever are not the illness, but the signs of a cold; so too my sins are signs of something more deeply wrong.

We speak of original sin, an illness that infects all humanity.

Traditionally we have said there are seven forms this illness takes, seven deadly sins that underlie our sinful actions and contaminate our good deeds. They are lust, wrath, gluttony, covetousness, envy, sloth and pride.

God has gifted us with creativity, a power we use most obviously through our sexuality. Lust leads us to use that gift selfishly. We use people for our own pleasure. Sometimes lust disguises itself as a drive to power that might not appear sexual at all. Artists, politicians and bosses are among those in danger of this sin, because power can be used creatively or selfishly. The sin of the schoolyard bully is lust.

We have dreams. They motivate us to pray and work for the Kingdom of God. However, when our dreams cannot be fulfilled, we can give in to anger and attack other people for the sake of our dream. The social reformer, the pacifist, the judge and the preacher must beware of this sin because the visionaries of what can be, when frustrated by what is, can turn wrathful.

God has given the things of the world as supports for our lives. Gluttony refuses to know limits in using them. We eat too much, we drink too much, we buy too much and we destroy the environment because we will not settle for "enough."

Covetousness is greed, the urge to stake an exclusive claim to what God has given for all. Since God has given the whole world, this sin is never satisfied. It wants more and more because it wants all. Theft and war usually are signs of this sin. So are fraud and cheating. It is the one deadly sin with a holiday of its own, celebrated when Christians commemorate Christ's birth.

People are children of God. Envy is the sin that says they must be mine instead, subservient to me. They must not have, be or do better than I. It is the sin underlying "sour grapes," possessive relationships and "cutting people down to size." Look at the smirk on the face of someone who has made another either cry or explode and you'll see envy's smile.

The sloth is such an inactive animal that algae grows on its fur. We think of the sin of sloth as inactivity, but laziness sometimes appears very active. It is the sin of "Who cares?" Rather than put effort into thought, prayer, duties, learning or relationships, we act like whirlwinds of activity. Couch potatoes and their busy neighbors may have much in common.

Pride is the titanic sin. The "unsinkable" steamship was an example of pride at work. "We can do anything!" It is also the titanic sin in that it is the greatest and the foundation for all sin. Pride is the sin that says humanity really does not need the real God. I can be god. All "-ism's" are prone to the sin of pride, including Catholicism. When we forget that sin marks and mars all our creations, pride, the sin that underlies all others, triumphs.

The Good News is that Jesus is with us children of sin to declare us children of God. In him, we "have redemption, the forgiveness of sins." Knowing that, we can love and then be truly like God. And like the woman in the Gospel, because we love the world will know we have been forgiven.

Twelfth Sunday of the Year (C)

We spend much of our lives answering questions. "What do you want to be when you grow up?" becomes "When will you ever grow up?" School examinations give way to the questions on various applications. Questions, questions. Today, even Jesus becomes a questioner. But, his question is the most important question anyone can ever be asked. "Who do you say that I am?"

We can usually give some sort of answer. "My catechism told me that you are the Son of God." "Some theologian says you are the existential encounter between the divine and the human." "A novelist says you are a man struggling to understand himself."

A priest in Kyoto, Japan, once met a taxi driver who had an interesting idea of the answer to the question. My friend got into the cab and asked to be taken to the church at such-and-such a place. Since Japanese cabbies are no less garrulous than those in any other part of the world, he struck up a conversation.

"You're one of those church people?"

"Yes, I am."

"Pardon my saying so, but you folks don't seem to be doing very well here in Japan. I mean, in movies and TV, the church is a big thing in other countries, but here you don't get many people to come, do you?"

"No, we don't."

"I can't understand it," the cabbie continued, "there must be something good about this Jesus guy that so many people in other places follow him. Maybe you're not getting the message across here the right way."

"That has crossed my mind."

"Pardon me for suggesting this, but maybe you should go to New York and meet this Jesus fellow and tell him what you're doing and find out if you've got it right."

The cab driver had an answer to the question of Jesus — he is someone who runs a religious business out of a big office in New York.

But, neither the taxi driver's answer nor those we learn from others really answers Jesus. The disciples gave answers that came from other people — "You're John the Baptist, Elijah or another of the prophets."

"But you — who do *you* say that I am?" In the final analysis, Jesus is not interested in opinions the disciples or we may have heard or read. He doesn't want to know what our mothers or teachers or preachers told us. He wants to know what we think. Or, more accurately, what we believe. Or, even more accurately, what *I* believe.

The word "believe" is not primarily concerned with an intellectual activity. It comes from an ancient phrase that means "to be in love." Even in Latin, the word that comes to us as "creed" originally meant "I give my heart."

"Who do you say that I am? How do you love me?"

So, who do I say that Jesus is? How do I love him? Of all the questions I have ever been asked or ever will be asked, this is the most important. It may even be the single question the Lord will ask of me when my life is judged.

What is the answer? I might say with Peter, "You are the Messiah of God!" But, those are Peter's words and I don't talk that way. I might say, "You are the one who has loved me more than all others ever could or would. You are my true friend." "You are the one who walks with me in pain and confusion." "You are the one who will heal my death." I am not sure how I will answer the question. Finding that answer may be part of my vocation as a Christian.

How do you answer Jesus? Who do *you* say that he is? Jesus is asking you.

Thirteenth Sunday of the Year (C)

The followers of Jesus two thousand years ago were not always an attractive group. That should be a great comfort for us today, because we moderns are not an especially attractive group either.

Oh, yes, we have had our saints and will have more. We have done and continue to do much good in the world. We have proclaimed the Good News throughout the world and continue to do so. Presumably, we will do so till the end of time. But, all in all, we must admit that our record as a community is not impressive.

But, let's get back to those original followers of Jesus. How were they unattractive?

For starters, let's look at James and John. Jesus is on his way to Jerusalem, going to the cross that will save the whole world. Samaritans along the way refuse him hospitality because of their prejudice against Jews. When James and John see this, they go beyond the Samaritans' inhospitality and suggest that the divine power that will save the world be used to destroy the whole village — men, women, children and goats. As if the disciples could manage to "call down fire from heaven" to toast bread, let alone a village!

Then, there are the folks who would follow Jesus once they have finished doing what they think more important, like fulfilling family obligations. Those people miss the fact that absolutely no worldly duty or desire, no matter how important, is more important than an immediate response to the Lord's call.

So, where are we in all this? Well, there is certainly too much of James and John in the world. The renewed nuclear arms race and the foot-dragging by the "old" nuclear powers when it comes to ridding the world of such weapons shows that we are very willing to entertain thoughts of calling down fire from the heavens.

Though our military powers really can call down fire from above, even those of us who still cannot toast bread without mechanical assistance have not grown beyond James and John. If I look into my heart, I find a sordid mass of resentments, vengeful thoughts, and a library of nasty things I "could have said" and a museum of nastier things I "should have done." How much of my conversation consists of attacks upon people who have offended me or who I think have offended me?

Yes, I am a member of the apostolic Church, a follower of James and John.

But, it does not stop there. I am also a follower of those people who were too busy or who had so many important alternatives to following Christ. I have a job. I have appointments. I have commitments to family and society. I have a reputation to uphold. I have relationships that need to be nurtured and enjoyed. I have to study. I need some rest. I have so many truly important things to do. And yes, I also have a lot of unimportant things to do that I like to think are important.

It is true that I have responsibilities to the world, to others and to myself that I cannot lightly abandon. The point is, though, that there are times in my life when it is clear that the Lord is calling upon me to do something else.

I am presented with a person in need. I read or hear the Word of God and feel a stirring within me that calls for new directions in my life. I spend time in quiet prayer, and my heart knows I am being invited to a new way of following Christ, perhaps by getting rid of the resentments and anger that make me like James and John. Do I abandon or delay my other responsibilities? Or, do I say, "Thanks, Lord, but I'm terribly busy right now. Perhaps next week"?

When the Lord calls us, it is because he wants a response in action from us *now*, not a minute from now, not an hour from now, not next week or next year. He does not call upon us by appointment. He will not be penciled into our over-full schedules.

The good thing about this is the fact that he will call us at the best time for achieving what he intends with our lives. Answering now means answering at the best opportunity — the best for us, for the world, for the Lord.

Fourteenth Sunday of the Year (C)

The Lord sent his disciples out "as lambs in the midst of wolves." What he commanded his disciples two thousand years ago, he also commands us to do today. We are supposed to be lambs among the wolves.

Of course, Jesus was referring not to the four-legged variety of wolf, but to the more dangerous two-legged kind. He thought wolfishness an apt description of such people. That may be an injustice to the canine wolves, but not, sad to say, to the human ones.

The Renaissance humanist Erasmus coined the epigram,"Human beings are to each other either gods or wolves." Divine or lupine — which are we? Which am I? What makes a two-legged wolf?

Wolves travel in packs. They hunt in packs. They prey upon the weak. An old caribou or a young deer has no chance against their attack. Neither has a lamb. Wolves use remorseless cunning and inexorable strength.

Sound familiar? Most of history is about the strong swallowing the weak. Strong nations draw resources, wealth and life from weaker ones. Our social and economic structures favor the strong at the expense of the weak. Even in our homes and personal relationships, we engage in domestic devouring, acting out of strength, forcing our will upon others. From children in a playground to nations at war, the strong form packs, and woe to the weak.

How have we disciples fared? Not the way one would expect. Jesus sent us out as lambs, and we have, for the most part, not been devoured. Why is that?

Could it be that we convert the wolves? All one need do is look around to see that is not the case. Actually, something else has happened. We have learned to live like the wolves. We are sheep in wolves' clothing.

Church history is in part the story of the tensions that have marked and marred our community since the time of Jesus. We have compromised, we have accepted the protection of the world's power, we have blessed and even wielded that power.

I, too, have hidden my lamb-ness. I do what I must to fit in. After all, I know what happened to the Lamb of God — they crucified him. I avoid any danger of that happening to me. I go to church and say my prayers, but outside I keep quiet lest I attract attention from the wolves. So long as I am with the flock, I am fine. But Monday morning puts me back in the woods with the wolves. So, when I'm not with the flock baaing out hymns, I imitate the howls of the wolves.

The result is that the world is short-changed. Christ knows what the world is to be, what humanity should look like — lambs. If the world is not rescued from wolfishness, it is not ready to be part of the Kingdom of God. Jesus sent the seventy-two out to save the wolves, to help them become lambs.

We must teach the world's wolves a new way of living. We must teach respect for the weak and service to them. We must teach the wolves that lambs are not for devouring, but for showing us something about God.

We cannot do this unless we are willing to risk being eaten up. That is what the wolves did to Jesus. He talks to his lambs about the rejection we will face in our mission. It appears we will either be rejected by the wolves (except as a meal), or rejected by the Lord. Not much of a choice. Perhaps it is wiser for the time being to masquerade as wolves.

But, we know deep down that we cannot play wolf. We have been baptized in Christ, the Lamb of God. So, we cannot even be good at wolfishness because in our hearts we know we are really lambs.

Jesus is so impractical. When he sent the disciples, he should have told them to wear armor, to carry weapons, to acquire wisdom in the ways of the world. Instead, he told them to expect to meet wolves.

And then, an interesting thing happened. The disciples brought peace with them where they went. They defeated the powers of hell, casting out demons. Some lambs! That's who we really are, if we be willing to give up our own wolfishness, be willing to walk through the world as servants.

Fifteenth Sunday of the Year (C)

Perhaps the biggest hero in the story of the Good Samaritan is not a fictional character in the parable, but the real person who questioned Jesus, the lawyer.

In Jesus' day, there were two groups of Pharisees. The group Jesus had disputes with was rigorous in its interpretation of the Law. If God has given laws to the people, those laws must be observed in their entirety. As they say, "God did not offer Moses the Ten Suggestions."

However, there was another school of thought which said, in effect, that God's Law was an outline for life and that people had to use faith, love and common sense in applying the Law. The evidence in the Gospels is that Jesus got along well with that group.

The lawyer's question, "Teacher, what must I do to inherit everlasting life?" was one that anyone would ask in order to find out what side of the argument a teacher stood for. Jesus turns the question back to the lawyer: "What is written in the law? How do *you* read it?"

The lawyer gives the non-rigorist answer. There are 613 laws in the Bible, but they boil down to two in accord with which all the others are to be judged and lived. Love God and love your neighbor. Jesus commends the lawyer, showing which side he himself tended to favor, though he later says, in effect, that it, too, is wrong.

The lawyer isn't finished. He wants to know how broad the definition of neighbor should be.

The priest and the Levite who passed the injured man were not bad. They were obeying the Law of God. Their duties at the temple required that they remain ritually pure. Contact with blood or with a non-believer would make them incapable of serving God's people in the liturgy until they had undergone purification. The injured stranger might be a heathen. He might be a leper. He might bleed on them. They owed it to their vocation to avoid him. They may have said a prayer on his behalf as they passed — the way I might when I pass a beggar on the street. They did what the Law seemed to require of them.

The Samaritan was not bound by the same rules as the priest or Levite. He was not even a Jew. Being outside of the Law, he was free to respond to the call of his heart.

Now, imagine the lawyer hearing this. He is not a rigorous follower of the Law, but he is no Samaritan, either. He would obey the Law, but would adapt his obedience to circumstances. It would be natural for him upon hearing Jesus to become a defense lawyer, offering some explanation on behalf of the priest and Levite. He might have complained that the right thing was done by someone totally outside the Law. He might have resented the implication that his own position on the Law took second place to lawlessness.

But, he did not. When Jesus asks him to react to the story, he merely answers the question about neighborliness. Jesus, in effect, told the lawyer that the law does not really matter. It's like telling a baker that bread does not matter. The lawyer did not dispute that; he was a hero. He was ready to be told by Jesus, "Go and do the same."

What about me? Do I live by the rules? Do I look at every situation and ask what the law of God or the Church or the laws and customs of my society demand of me? Do I run my life according to the unwritten law of "What will the neighbors think?" Do I decide that my role as student, worker, spouse, parent, priest, man, woman or child should be the main consideration when I am faced with a situation that demands some response from me?

Jesus ran afoul of the religious authorities in part because in their dispute among themselves about how to live the Law he did not take sides so much as he rejected the whole premise of the argument.

As followers of Jesus, we are commissioned by him to serve any need we see, no matter what reasons we think there may be for passing by. When it comes to our brothers and sisters at the side of the road we travel through life, absolutely nothing should hinder us in being brothers or sisters — neighbors — to them.

Sixteenth Sunday of the Year (C)

When I was a boy, an old-fashioned gentleman who was related to our family through marriage would make it a point to politely stand whenever a woman entered the room. He certainly got a lot of exercise as my mother and aunts ran in and out of the room trying to corral a herd of unruly kids.

Posture is important. We tell children to stand up straight. Soldiers stand at attention when a superior speaks to them. In civilian society, citizens are expected to stand during their national anthem. At various times in the liturgy, we sit, stand, bow, genuflect or kneel. When a bishop or priest preaches, he can either stand, or sit in the presider's chair as Jesus did in the synagogue.

In the story about Jesus in the home of Martha and Mary, Mary's posture is important. In fact, it is the key to understanding not only the account, but a sign of an important point about those whom Christ calls. According to Luke, Mary "sat beside the Lord at his feet listening to him speak."

Over the years, the difference between Martha and Mary has been used to contrast the so-called "active" life with a life of quiet contemplation, especially for women, and claiming that passive attentiveness, symbolized by Mary, is holier than action, epitomized by Martha.

But, the story is not about that. To see what Jesus was doing in that house we need not concern ourselves with dinner preparations. We must look at Mary's posture.

She was sitting at the feet of Jesus. In the world in which Jesus lived and taught, that posture had a very special meaning, a meaning that those who saw it and those who originally read Luke's Gospel would have understood. And that meaning would have surprised or even shocked them. It clearly bothered Martha.

The ones who sat at the feet of a teacher were that teacher's disciples. We still speak of a disciple sitting at the feet of a master. Mary was a disciple of Jesus, entitled to sit at his feet as any other disciple would.

But in that time and place, women belonged in the kitchen, doing what Martha was doing, For a woman to be occupying the position of a full disciple was a radical challenge to the society in which Jesus lived. Mary was claiming equality with men! And Jesus not only allowed it; he even said to Martha that Mary had "chosen the better part." And, he added, "it will not be taken from her."

In fact, though, not much time passed before it was taken from those women who followed Mary as disciples of Christ. In St. Paul's authentic letters, as opposed to those written in his name after his death, we even see women in leadership roles in various communities. But, Jesus' and the early church's radical view of women's equality with men did not long survive. The force of customary attitudes toward women, even on the part of women, was just too strong. It remains strong, though throughout the history of the church exceptional women like St. Catherine of Siena in the 14th Century have managed to play forthrightly leading roles in our community.

Today, as the attitudes toward women that subverted the practice of Jesus are changing in many places, we in the church are being challenged to once again accept the fact that Jesus still has something to teach us that seems subversive of the so-called "normal" ordering of society and the church.

Today, those who want to restore the equality that Jesus taught are attacked as "radical feminists" without that charge being really defined. But, the first radical feminist in the history of our faith was Jesus himself.

So, the question we all — male and female alike — are forced to ask ourselves is: What do we do as individuals and as a church that betrays Mary's vocation to full discipleship, and what must we do to recapture this important aspect of what Jesus meant his followers to be?

Seventeenth Sunday of the Year (C)

Do you pray as well as you wish? I don't mean, "When you pray for something, do you get it?" The answer to our prayers is up to God, and though God always answers our prayers, we know that sometimes the answer is, "No."

I mean, when you pray, do you really feel that, as the old catechism definition put it very inadequately, that you are "lifting up your mind and heart to God"?

In today's Gospel, one of the disciples sees a chance to find the formula. Jesus has been praying. The disciple realizes there is something about the prayer of Jesus that seems to make it a deeper communion with God than the disciple thought himself or herself capable of.

So, the disciple approaches Jesus and says, "Lord, teach us to pray as John taught his disciples." A rabbi usually taught his disciples prayers they could use as a way of bringing his teaching into their prayer. And Jesus does it, teaching a prayer that has become the hallmark of his disciples through all ages in all places and among all the different groups that call him Lord.

Having taught the words, though, Jesus goes on to say that they are not really all that important.

Our problem (and this is where the catechism definition was misleading) is that we think that praying is primarily something that we do. It is, of course, something we do, but what we do is not the most important thing. Prayer is our relationship with God. God is the chief actor.

When I focus upon myself and what I do in prayer, I become so caught up in formulas, postures, breathing exercises and such that I forget that the whole reason I pray is to remember who God is, and within that relationship, who I am.

Jesus gives us two important lessons as a commentary upon the disciple's request.

The first is a story about someone awakened in the night by a neighbor who needs bread. At first, the groggy one is unwilling to help. However, eventually he gets up and helps his neighbor, if only to get back to sleep.

"So I say to you, ask, and it will be given you; search, and you will find; knock, and the door will be opened for you. For everyone who asks receives, and everyone who searches finds, and for everyone who knocks the door will be opened."

What Jesus is telling us is that the important thing about our prayer is not so much *how* we do it as *that* we do it. God will hear us.

If sleepyheads like us respond to prayers addressed to us, we can be sure that God will hear us and respond. Therefore, we can and should pray with confidence. The first principle of prayer is that God will always hear us and respond.

Jesus' second point is, perhaps, more important to those of us who worry about praying well or properly. He uses examples to teach us.

The first example is of a child asking a parent for a fish. In such a case, the child will not receive a snake. The second example is of the child asking for an egg. The child need not worry about getting a scorpion.

On one level, Jesus is telling us that when we pray we need not worry that God will do evil to us in response to our needs. God does not tease. But, there is another level to what he says. It involves puns.

In the Aramaic Jesus and his disciples spoke, the words for "fish" and "snake" and the words for "egg" and "scorpion" sounded similar. Perhaps there were even situations where mixups could occur: for example, when someone, warned that there was a scorpion in a basket, reached in planning to make an omelet.

Jesus is telling us disciples that we need not worry that God will not understand our prayers. We do not have to use proper formulas, the right words. God loves us so much that our inadequate prayers suffice. In other words, the disciple's anxiety to learn the right words to use in prayer was misplaced. There are no right words; there are no wrong words. God will not misunderstand us.

So, what need we do? Pray.

Eighteenth Sunday of the Year (C)

In ancient times, the wealth of Croesus was legendary. Midas had so much money that a legend grew up that all he touched turned to gold. Today, I suppose, we would talk of Bill Gates as a modern legend of wealth. Some day, he will have as much as Croesus and Midas have — nothing. You and I will have the same amount.

That simple fact is what makes greed so foolish. It is the reason that in the parable, God calls the rich man, "You fool!" Jesus warned us that "one's possessions do not guarantee life."

In the Gospel today, greed is for wealth. The man who approached Jesus wanted his share of an inheritance. The man in the parable wanted "the good life," a life of physical comfort and ease.

But, there are other things for which we can be greedy. In fact, greed for money and goods may be less destructive of my humanity than some other greedy desires. I want to look good, both physically and socially. That's not wrong in itself, but if I am willing to sacrifice health or common sense to that desire, something is definitely wrong.

I want status; I want to win; I want recognition; I want special treatment. I want it ALL. But Jesus says, "avoid greed in *all* its forms."

The 18th Century English poet Matthew Green wrote of "avarice, the sphincter of the heart." Sphincters are muscles that close off openings in the body. They squeeze shut so that nothing can get out.

That is what greed does to me. It squeezes my heart shut. When I act out of greed, I act for myself. At the very least, I put others second or forget or ignore them. At the very worst, I destroy them on my way to what I want. My heart is so squeezed that no love can get out. Or in.

Jesus is upset by greed because it deprives us of true godliness. There are many ways in which I can be godlike in my own minor way. I can create. I can think. But, most of all, I can love. Greed squeezes shut my ability to love God or others. When I am busy grabbing what I can get or holding on to what I have gotten, my hands are not free to give, nor are they open to receive. "Avoid greed in all its forms, because one's possessions do not guarantee life."

The love of God guarantees life. Might it be that I am greedy because deep down I am not yet ready to rely upon the love of God? Do I really believe that this world is the whole story? If this world is all there be, then greed is a way of trying to guarantee my life.

If I have it all, at least I will have something to show for having been born. If there be nothing more for me than what I can get my hands on, then greed is common sense. My fame and fortune may not outlast me, but I won't care. As long as I have them, I know I am still alive. Perhaps I am greedy because I fear death. Greed is another name for fear. If I have things (whether tangible or intangible) I know I am alive.

Greed can never stop. Since in my heart I want to live forever, my desire for things that hide death is endless. I will never have enough.

No matter how much of my greed is satisfied (and it will never be fully satisfied), my life will end. My possessions are like a blindfold, hiding death from me. But they will not hide me from death. It will come and I will have nothing.

What can I do? I know that greed is something that puts barriers between myself and God, myself and others. But, I also need it as proof that my life is real, that it has value, even if measured by transitory standards of gold and glory.

The remedy is, perhaps, a willingness to not hide from death. When I really accept death as truly the entrance to a new, deeper experience of God's life-giving love, then I can live without greed. I can allow death to kill my greed before either greed or death kills me.

Nineteenth Sunday of the Year (C)

At every Mass, following the Lord's Prayer, the priest adds a prayer that says that "we wait in joyful hope." Day after day, year after year, century after century, millennium after millennium we wait for — for what? for whom? Is there really a Savior, a God, to come after all?

Are we deluding ourselves? Are we like the tramps in Beckett's play *Waiting for Godot*, pathetic characters in an absurd world waiting and waiting for no reason for someone who will never come?

One way we have dealt with the problem of waiting is to forget that we are waiting at all. Like the servant in the parable, we say to ourselves, "My master is taking his time about coming." We occupy ourselves with all sorts of distractions of the moment, many of them truly worthwhile, but distractions none the less. We serve the world, we worship, we study. We organize an entire Church.

But, today's Gospel reminds us that regardless of whatever else we may do in the interim, we are waiting. The servants may have a dance party while awaiting the master's return, but they still keep an eye out for that return.

So, where is he? Where is the Savior for whom we "wait in joyful hope" or bored resignation or inattentive activity?

We may say that the Lord comes to us in various ways throughout our lives. We say that we encounter him in prayer or that we see him in our neighbor; we hear him speak in Scripture; we share his life in the Eucharist — provided, that is, that we have the faith to either hear or see him at such times. But, are we deluding ourselves, taking refuge from the possibility that he may never come by making believe he comes all the time?

Momentary, faith-dependent comings are not the coming of which Jesus spoke. They are not the coming for which we wait.

What we await is a different sort of coming, an absolutely unambiguous coming that means a perpetual presence with us. And that is yet to happen. Or, so it seems.

What is waiting? What do we do when we wait for someone to come to us or contact us? If it is someone we are anxious to meet, we try to kill time, but without much success. We pick up a book or magazine, but keep looking at the door, a window or the telephone. Our eyes move across the page, but our mouths could never tell what we "read" because our minds were not in the reading. We pace back and forth. We look at our watch over and over again. We turn on the TV and stare blankly at the screen.

In some ways, when we await someone, he or she is already present because the expectation of the coming is shaping our activities, our feelings and our attitudes. Whether we wait in hope or in dread, the thing or person or event we await has become a part of our life. In fact, we pay more attention to the person whom we await than we do to someone who is actually with us. The absent person we wait for becomes more real than the present person.

When we wait for Christ, he shapes us. If we really wait in expectation, he becomes more real to us than the "reality" we see around us. Perhaps that is what it means to wait in joyful hope for the coming of the Lord. In some sense, while we wait for him, he is with us. He is part of the waiting.

It is his presence with us as we wait that makes our Christian wait one of joyful hope. In our baptism, in prayer, in the Eucharist, in the community that gathers and waits in his name, he is with us.

Waiting is a key part of the Christian vocation. When we "wait in joyful hope" there is a real presence of the Lord for us. If we lose the sense of expectation, lose the urge to cry out, "Come, Lord Jesus!" our faith will become a mere matter of ceremonies, words and gestures. It will become absurd, and Jesus will sooner or later become for us no more real than Godot.

So, we keep expecting the unambiguous coming of the Lord. We may have to wait millennia. No matter. We will wait with and for the Lord.

Twentieth Sunday of the Year (C)

From about January 588 BC till July 587, Jerusalem was surrounded by the Babylonian army of King Nebuchadnezzar II. As the siege continued, starvation and disease began to claim lives. According to the Book of Lamentations, mothers even cooked their own children for food. People knew that the fall of a city always resulted in murder, rape, pillage, arson and slavery. Their only hope was in the troops who manned the walls, fighting off attacks, shooting arrows into the besieging troops.

Before the war, Jeremiah warned that it was a mistake to revolt against Babylon, which had earlier conquered the country and installed Zedekiah as ruler. Even after war began, Jeremiah did not keep quiet. He continued to issue his jeremiads against King Zedekiah, his advisors and his policies. In a country at war, in a city under siege, that is treason. Jeremiah's predictions of defeat were demoralizing the troops. So, he was dumped into a muddy well. This would mean his death, but no one would be directly responsible for spilling his blood.

So far, this is a story that could happen — and has happened — in many countries. Even in times of peace, authorities do not take kindly to attacks upon their policies. When it becomes apparent that their policies are disastrous, they are even more inclined to silence nay-sayers. Zedekiah and his princes have disciples all over the world.

But, the story takes a strange turn. Ebed-melech goes to the king and says, "these men have been at fault in all they have done to the prophet Jeremiah. He will die of famine on the spot, for there is no more food in the city."

King Zedekiah relents and tells Ebed-melech to set Jeremiah free. Did the king figure that since everyone was starving anyway, it made no difference where Jeremiah did his starving? Did he feel that since all was lost and everyone knew it, whatever Jeremiah said or did could not really affect the already-demoralized defenders? We don't know. I think it had something to do with his recognition that Jeremiah was, indeed, a prophet, one who spoke for God.

Perhaps the king realized that those who speak for God will say what we do not wish to hear. God's word will always be treasonous to the ways of the world.

In the Gospel, Jesus declares himself to be like Jeremiah, a bearer of what seems to be bad news. "Do you think that I have come to bring peace to the earth? No, I tell you, but rather division!"

People in Jerusalem did not relish Jeremiah's pronouncements. Neither do we relish hearing Jesus' saying that our families and society will be torn apart by dissension. The Jerusalemites wanted independence and food. We want peace and harmony. God seems to give what we do not want, and then expects us to call it "Good News."

Do you know the answer to the question: How do you train a mule? First, you take a large plank, and hit the animal over the head to get its attention. We are mulish, too self-contented, too dense and too self-absorbed to see that what God offers us goes far beyond anything that we are willing to settle for. Jeremiah and Jesus are saying, "Never mind what you think important. It will not last. In fact, it must not last so that you can receive what will last, God's eternal love." Sometimes, we need to feel a plank over the head to get the message.

What we think of as reality — the day-to-day world in which we sin, harm ourselves and others, regret but do little else about pain and injustice, forget God and eternity — this so-called "reality" is falsehood. True reality is found in the will of God, a will that calls for love received and shared, love that transcends time. It's a reality that we will only, it seems, turn to when we've been hit with a plank.

So, Jeremiah in his day and Jesus in his (which is ours) say that our dreams shall be shattered against the reality of God's love. It will hurt. It will hurt as much as slavery or strife. But, it shall free us from the delusion that this world offers what we really need. God offers what we really need, and shall do whatever is painfully necessary to smash anything that makes us willing to settle for less.

Twenty-First Sunday of the Year (C)

The person who asked Jesus, "Lord, will only a few be saved?" may have been concerned for the salvation of others, or just worrying whether or not there would be room for one more. As so often happens, Jesus does not give a clear, direct answer.

That has not stopped others from doing so. Jehovah's Witnesses teach that those who will go to heaven are limited to 144,000. There are approximately two billion Christians in the world today (among whom Jehovah's Witnesses are usually not counted). So if that figure were true it would lead to the Lord hearing a lot of us saying, "We ate and drank with you."

Though most Christians have been open to larger numbers of saved, they have not avoided speculating. Occasionally, one may be accosted on the street by another who asks, "Are you saved?" It is a not uncommon concern, and the question is probably asked of mirrors more than of strangers.

Many people give a confident "Yes!" as their answer. Others despairingly answer, "No." Some of the world's least attractive — and even repulsive — Christians are those who are so convinced of their salvation that they feel justified in belittling, persecuting and belaboring their "unsaved" neighbors. Some of the most heart-breaking Christians are those who are so convinced of their damnation that they forget the whole premise of salvation — God's forgiving love. The correct answer to "Are you saved?" is probably some variation of "I don't know, but, God willing, I am."

But, the answer is not important because the question is not important. Speculation is a waste of time. If my salvation is related to how I spend my short time on earth, I have more important things to do than to speculate on how God's love will ultimately deal with me.

So, Jesus shifts the question. He does not say who is saved, but tells his listeners to act. Rather than speculation, God wants action. Instead of wondering who is saved, and whether or not I am among them, I should be living a particular kind of life.

Those who "stand outside and knock at the door, saying, 'Lord, open to us'" are rejected as "evildoers." They feel they deserve a place in the Kingdom of God because they have eaten and drunk with the Lord. He says he does not even know them.

More important than our membership in the community of those who know the Lord is that we not be evildoers. We must be "good-doers."

The good-doers who will have a place among the saved need not be members of the community of faith at all. "People will come from east and west, from north and south, and will eat in the kingdom of God." How one lives, rather than how one believes, will be the important factor.

So, how do I become a good-doer? A burning interest in my own salvation will not suffice. It may even interfere because good-doers must be focused upon others, not themselves. Ironically, the best assurance of my salvation is a lack of concern with my salvation.

Instead, what I need is to spend my time and energy for the salvation of others. Does that mean I should accost folks on the street to ask about their salvational status? No. Salvation is the state of being fully what God intends one to be. What God intends is loving communion with each of us and for us to live in communion with one another.

So, whatever I do that helps my brothers and sisters know God's love and share it is an aid to their salvation. And my brothers and sisters are all people. The best way for them to know the love of God is, of course, to see it in the people who can turn to Christ and say, "We ate and we drank with you and heard your teaching." I must show practical, here-and-now love to my neighbor, responding to what he or she (not I) thinks are the areas of life that need help, need love.

If we live that way, the Lord's word to us will be, "Of course I know you. You have been with me all along, but were too busy loving others to notice. You were more concerned with helping others become the image of my Father than you were with your own salvation. Welcome!"

Twenty-Second Sunday of the Year (C)

A symposium, for me, is a dull affair where opinionated people peddle their opinions. There is a lot of talking *at*, but little listening *to* or talking *with*. Perhaps I have never had the good fortune to attend a good symposium. There should be such things, because the word *symposium* means a good time.

Its ancestry is Greek, a combination of the prefix *syn-*, meaning "together" and the word meaning "drink." Originally, a symposium was a gathering of people who discussed intellectual matters while drinking wine. More than their professors at dull conferences, students who attempt to solve the world's problems while seated around a pizza and a pitcher of beer (or their local equivalents) are carrying on a venerable tradition, the roots of the university.

In today's Gospel, Jesus is at a symposium. Scholars say that Luke took various sayings and deeds of Jesus that he thought belonged together and presented them as happening during a meal. Perhaps it was Luke's Greek background that gave him the idea of presenting Jesus at a symposium.

It is a Friday night or Saturday daytime. People are sprawled around the floor, leaning on cushions. (Chairs were not common, and people ate around a low table.) There is wine, food and lots of talk. As Luke says, all eyes were on Jesus. What he said or did would form the basis of the symposium.

Today, we hear two topics. In the first, Jesus comments upon those jockeying for good places at the table. At first, he merely gives the kind of advice that any teacher might give. "When you are invited, go and sit at the lowest place, so that when your host comes, he may say to you, 'Friend, move up higher'; then you will be honored in the presence of all who sit at the table with you."

This is not very profound advice. In fact, it seems calculating. I have seen people follow it literally, and their reasons have nothing to do with humility. But, Jesus adds something that puts his advice in a new light. He is not teaching manners or social advancement, but the Kingdom of God. The host parallels God, who invites all people to a banquet.

My place at that banquet is not one I have earned. It is for God to decide where I belong. It is in humility that I know my littleness. It is in humility that I can listen to the voice of God. It is in humility that I know that all I have comes from God. "For all who exalt themselves will be humbled, and those who humble themselves will be exalted."

As the eating and drinking continue, so does the symposium.

Sometime later in the meal (and just because Luke puts one saying of Jesus after another does not mean we cannot imagine more conversation and joking in between), Jesus turns to his host and makes an observation about invitations. "When you give a banquet, invite the poor, the crippled, the lame, and the blind."

In a time and place without social welfare schemes, the disabled were almost invariably poor. They were frequently outcasts because some people thought their disabilities were a divine punishment. So, Jesus is not talking so much about physical disabilities as he is about the poor and the outcast. He tells the host to invite them.

On one level, Jesus is recommending charity to those most in need. But, he is also issuing an invitation to the host and to us. He is inviting us to be like God who invites all people to the banquet of eternal life-giving love. In so doing, we show God's love to our neighbor. Through us, our neighbors will know God. We also show ourselves ready to understand and receive God's gift. "You will be blessed, because they cannot repay you, for you will be repaid at the resurrection of the righteous."

In Luke's Gospel, the symposium continues. It should continue in our lives. We tend to think that reflection upon the Word of God, upon the Work of God, is something solemn, serious, and private.

But, sometimes, we should be ready to hear the Word in the hustle and bustle of our lives, in the symposium of eating, drinking and gabbing that is our daily life.

Twenty-Third Sunday of the Year (C)

Luke says that "large crowds were traveling" with Jesus. But, he turns to them and says things that seem calculated to drive them away.

"Whoever comes to me and does not hate father and mother, wife and children, brothers and sisters, yes, and even life itself, cannot be my disciple." In the idiom of those days, "hate" could mean "not prefer." So, the crowd would have understood Jesus to mean, "Whoever prefers father and mother...."

Even if his listeners could put Jesus ahead of parents, spouses, children and relations, putting him ahead of "life itself" is a big order. It is easy to imagine folks answering, "Uh, Okay. Well, so long."

Jesus continues, almost as if he wanted to drive off those who had not yet left. "Whoever does not carry the cross and follow me cannot be my disciple." Those folks knew about crosses. A cross was one of the most cruel tortures ever devised, and some of the people with Jesus may have seen it. So, more may have said, "Gotta go!"

Apparently, there were still some brave souls left, because Jesus continues his discouraging words. Before deciding to follow him, one should weigh up the consequences. What, exactly, will it cost to follow Jesus?

He finishes up by saying, "So therefore, none of you can become my disciple if you do not give up all your possessions." That includes such "possessions" as wealth, family and even life. That is a steep price to pay.

Some people do choose to prefer Jesus over father, mother, spouse and all the rest. Some of them choose Jesus over life itself. Even in Christian families and communities, a decision to follow Christ more whole-heartedly can provoke opposition, tears and ostracism.

What about me? Have I done anything lately because of my faith that at least raised eyebrows? Has being a disciple of Jesus cost me anything beyond what I might put into the collection basket at church? Probably not, and there are two possible reasons for that.

The first may be that I have been lukewarm in my faith. Perhaps I have not made any choices lately that would put my faith in conflict with the world. Perhaps I even continue to call myself a Christian simply in order to avoid problems with fathers, mothers and others.

But, there may be another reason I have not made any hard choices. Perhaps I have not yet been presented with a situation in which I have had to make a really difficult choice to live as a Christian. I think that is what Jesus' examples today remind us. Obviously, every moment of the Christian life is not a call to martyrdom or heroic virtue. Usually, the Christian life consists of getting from wake-up in the morning to bed-down in the evening while trying to live the unheroic virtues.

Jesus tells of a builder estimating costs and a king weighing his resources for war. A builder does not put up a skyscraper or even a pig sty every day. Even the most warlike rulers have days of armistice, if not peace. They plan for the special situations. Jesus is telling us to do the same.

If we embark upon the Christian life, there will be many times of calm. There will be times when our faith seems no big challenge to us or the world. But, if we "sign on" for the life of a disciple, we must know that we may be called upon at any moment to make big decisions, to take radical actions that may turn our lives upside down.

I once spoke with a man who was the only Christian in the Tokyo fire department. He said his work was like his Christian vocation, because at any moment he might be called upon to give his life for the sake of others.

We are like firefighters. They may be sitting around watching TV together or cooking a meal. But, they know that at any moment they may be called to face unknown dangers, to risk their lives. A training program for firefighters that did not mention anything about fires would be a very strange one. Today, Jesus is telling us to be ready for fire so that when it comes, we will not be surprised, but resolute, knowing that the crisis today is one we took into account from the start.

Twenty-Fourth Sunday of the Year (C)

A lost sheep drops to the ground and refuses to move. The shepherd who finds it must pick the beast up. There is no other way to get it back to the flock. It must be carried.

Sheep are too big to carry under one's arm, so a fireman's carry (across the shoulders) is the only way to do it. Since in Jesus' world a lost sheep was probably in a rocky desert, a shepherd staggering along with one on his shoulders would have risked sprained ankles or worse.

If I were a shepherd and one of my sheep wandered off, I would say, "Tough luck," and leave it at that.

Of course, the sheep would have some right to complain: "You say *I* don't understand when I'm being helped, but you're no better. God does all sorts of things in your life, sends you all sorts of people, teachings and opportunities, and you complain or ignore them! You would rather sit down in your stupidity, your sin and your laziness than get up and follow the Lord, even though he is leading you to safety."

Let's leave the sheep (they are getting embarrassing) and turn to money. That's something we all appreciate.

The lost coin to which Jesus refers is not merely loose change dropped by the woman while unpacking the groceries. A woman wore her wealth as a headdress, the coins strung around her brow. The woman in the story has only ten coins, each worth about one day's wage. With only that much of an emergency fund, she is poor. To lose even a single coin is a disaster.

So, she gets to work. In a house without windows, she has to rely on the light that comes through the door and a small flickering oil lamp. Her broom would be her major help. By sweeping the whole place, she might hear a welcome "clink" as the broom hit the coin and knocked it against something.

In both stories, of course, the searcher is God. God is the shepherd who will not leave the sheep to die in its stupidity. He searches us out and then does the real work of saving us from ourselves, saving us for our real home with the flock of God.

God is the woman who looks for the lost coin. (Jesus had no trouble speaking of God as a woman and the early Church had no trouble passing on the tradition that he did so, something that might shock many today.)

God will do all in her power to bring us back to her. We can lose ourselves in all the dark places of the world and of our hearts, but she will be persistent.

And finally, God is the loving father who embraces his wayward son and welcomes him home to a feast.

Why? Why should God take such trouble with me? I am not worth the effort. I am stupid, wandering away from the way I know leads to full life. I am lost more often than not. Or, rather, I lose myself. Yet, God keeps coming after me, offering forgiveness and wisdom. The reason could not be in myself. Someone so perverse as I cannot deserve God's searching love, but I receive it all the same. It can only be because God loves me regardless of how I act.

I tend to view the Christian life as a project, something to be achieved. We draw up lists of things to do — work for justice, say our prayers, share the Eucharist, contribute to charity (and the collection basket).

All of that is nonsense compared to what Christianity is really all about — God the shepherd who will never abandon me when I stray. God the housewife who will search me out wherever I may get lost. God the father who will always forgive and welcome me.

I am the lost sheep, but God will lift me up on his shoulders and bring me home. I am the lost coin, but God will hunt me down till she holds me once again. I am the wandering son, but God welcomes me home.

This is the Gospel. One scholar describes today's passage as "the distilled essence of the good news, the gospel within the Gospel." God is merciful not to "humankind," but to lost, bewildered, stupid, unlovable me!

Twenty-Fifth Sunday of the Year (C)

St. Jerome wrote: "Our walls glitter with gold and gold gleams upon our ceilings and the capitals of our pillars; yet Christ is dying at our doors in the person of his poor, naked and hungry." About 1600 years have passed, but though tastes have changed, Christ remains at our doors.

Whether our churches be decorated by Michelangelo or from mail-order catalogues, whether our homes be estates or hovels, whether our clothing be designer jeans or hand-me-downs, we have never given worldly goods the treatment they deserve. Or, rather, the use they deserve.

Jesus speaks of "dishonest wealth." His presupposition is that wealth is something that stands against the justice of God. But, Jesus recognizes that possessions are a normal part of life, and that some, whether by fair means or foul, will have more than others. As he so often does, Jesus shifts the focus. Here, he shifts it from possession to use.

"Make friends for yourselves with dishonest wealth, so that when it fails, you will be welcomed into eternal dwellings."

Wealth will go. Economies collapse, buildings crumble, clothes go out of fashion, we die. "A fool and his money are soon parted," says the proverb. In fact, whether we be foolish or wise, sooner or later we and our wealth will be parted. We have no choice in that matter.

We do, however, have some choice in the way we and our possessions are separated. We can wait until they are taken, or we can share them with others, with "Christ at our doors."

Who are the "friends" who will give us an everlasting reception? In the parable of the dishonest manager, it is debtors, those who need relief. In other words, it is the poor. If I wish to "buy" a place in "the eternal dwellings," I must, in a sense, bribe the reception committee, the poor.

I have possessions, but they are "mine" only for the sake of aiding those in need. As Francis Bacon said more than 300 years ago, "Money is like muck, no good except it be spread." Jesus put it less picturesquely: "If you are not trustworthy with dishonest wealth, who will trust you with true wealth?"

Trustworthiness with riches means using them for those who need them and what they can do. If I so use them, then the poor will stand at the gates of heaven and say as I approach, "Oh, it's you! Come on in — and thanks again."

Does that mean that I should give up everything? It may, indeed, mean so. The Church has always presented that as an ideal, though we have never lived it successfully. It's embarrassing to think of how much we spend on crucifixes or Christmas stables while Christ remains at the doors of our cathedrals, churches and homes. Some of us take vows to live in poverty for the sake of others. Seldom, however, does "religious poverty" involve the rigor, suffering and lack of security of the truly poor.

Such problems do not belong only to the church at large or to certain people in it. It is a problem for a very specific Christian, myself. I am afraid to let go. I want security for my future. I want a bit of comfort in the present. I want to enjoy what my possessions — wealth, time, talents, health, life — enable me to do. What can I do about that?

Perhaps the dishonest manager in the parable gives a hint. He makes an "investment" in hopes of reaping later benefits. Investing is a way to wealth in much of the world today. Ideally, an investment grows, leading to yet further investment. Can I do that with my possessions, putting at least some of them forward for the needy?

But, how big an investment is enough? I'm not likely to invest all that I have for the poor. The opposite is the danger; I might not invest enough to profit. There is a simple rule of thumb: it should be at least inconvenient. There should be something I would like to do with my treasure, time or talent that I will not be able to do because I have offered them to the poor.

If I can do that, I may find that the return on my investment enables me, or even impels me, to do more and one day buys my way past the gate-keeping poor of heaven. That may be getting in by hook or by crook, but remember that the Master ultimately commends the devious manager.

Twenty-Sixth Sunday of the Year (C)

Am I the rich man or Lazarus? I do not consider myself rich, but compared to most of the world's people, I have incredible wealth.

That wealth is not merely monetary. It is also psychological (I live among friends and with a high degree of personal security), intellectual (I can read and write), physical (my health is protected by preventive and healing care), social (I live in a peaceful place and can exercise a high level of freedom) and spiritual (I have been called to know God's love in Jesus Christ). There is no doubt about it — I am the rich man.

In that case, it is important that I know where he went wrong — unless, of course, I am willing to risk baking in "the abode of the dead."

We should not take that risk lightly. Jesus talks on several occasions about those who will be cast off from God. In that light, today's parable is especially frightening, because the hell-bound rich man and I have so much in common.

So, what was the rich man's problem? Was it wealth? No, he is never criticized for that, nor is there any reason to think that he is condemned because of how he acquired it. Was the rich man cruel? Did he oppress Lazarus? Did he call the authorities to have the beggar removed from his gate? No, he did none of these things. In fact, he did nothing at all regarding Lazarus.

That was the problem. The rich man at his table may not have even been aware of the beggar at his gate. The rich man would have been busy with his day-to-day concerns, just as I am. He may not have even had time to go outside. Even if he did, he might not have noticed one more beggar in a world full of beggars. The rich man did not know Lazarus.

Mother Teresa offered an excuse in such circumstances. "The trouble is that rich people, well-to-do people, very often don't really know who the poor are; and that is why we can forgive them, for knowledge can only lead to love, and love to service. And so, if they are not touched by them, it's because they do not know them."

Mother Teresa was more generous than Abraham — or Jesus. When the rich man begs Abraham to send Lazarus to end his brothers' ignorance, he is refused. Ignorance is no excuse because there is no excuse for ignorance.

This brings us to the core of the rich man's (and my) problem. There is simply no excuse for not seeing Lazarus.

The rich man was indifferent to the world outside his gate. The walls of his house were the walls of his world. Such walls need not be a house, either. We build walls of family, race, nationality, class, religion, education, neighborhood and the devil-knows-what else that shut out some part of the world, some Lazarus.

There is no excuse. God gives us a whole world, and if we close our eyes to any part of it, we are refusing God. We make our private world so small that we cannot see either the good God does or the evil we must combat.

What can I do? I am, without doubt, the rich man of the parable. Am I doomed to hell?

There are signs of hope. The first is that since living in communion with all the world's people in Christ is what I was created for, it may be easier to know and care about my brothers and sisters than it is to close them out of my world.

Another is my discomfort. The rich man came to his senses and saw Lazarus too late for it to do him any good. This parable is a wake-up call to see that each and every man and woman is a child of God, and therefore my brother, my sister. Awareness can be the first step in conversion.

And what will conversion look like? It may be as simple as exercising good manners to strangers I meet, including shop clerks and others who serve me. It may be paying closer attention to news reports of what is happening to my brothers and sisters around the world. It may be learning about other cultures, customs and religions. It may be sacrificing some of my psychological, intellectual, physical, social, material and spiritual wealth for the sake of others.

It will be living in the real world, the whole real world.

Twenty-Seventh Sunday of the Year (C)

Palestinian Jews two thousand years ago tended to exaggerate when they spoke, so it was natural that Jesus would, too. Therefore, despite what Jesus says, anyone who wants to move a sycamore to the sea should use a chain saw, a crane and a heavy-duty truck instead of prayer.

If flying sycamores are an example of Palestinian exaggeration, can we write off Jesus' words and look for more "truthful" passages? No, if Jesus exaggerated, it was because he wanted to make an impression, wanted folks to pay attention to what he said. So, what about using a mustard seed to move a sycamore? What can it possibly mean?

The disciples ask Jesus to do something we, too, ask: "Increase our faith." We see the horrors of the world around us and wonder if there really could be a God who cares. Our cultures are increasingly becoming "post-religious," with decisions in the political, social and economic realms made without reference to any beliefs at all. Some say that the rise of fundamentalism among Christians, Muslims, Hindus and others is a last gasp by panicked believers who see impending doom for their beliefs.

But, is the situation really all that new? Habakkuk faced the same problems some 2500 years ago. It never has been easy to believe. It never will be.

So we pray, "Increase my faith!"

Jesus' answer is not comforting. "If you had faith the size of a mustard seed..." Well, it seems that my faith is not even so big as such a small seed, because it doesn't suffice. I don't even want to shake, let alone move sycamores, I only want my heart to be moved. That shouldn't be harder than flinging trees into the ocean.

Perhaps Jesus is telling us that it is not a problem of amount. Perhaps we already have enough faith. A mustard seed's worth suffices, so perhaps we need not ask for an increased faith. There is something else needed to make us feel that our faith is alive.

That may be the reason Luke linked Jesus' words about faith with an admonition about service. Faith is not something we hold on to like a pocketful of seeds, something that can be increased by the mere asking. Faith is a form of service to God. The amount of faith is not important — a mustard seed's worth suffices. What matters is what we do with that faith, whether it be as small as a mustard seed or as big as a coconut.

Worrying about my faith is self-centered. It's as if faith existed for me and an increase in it increased my spiritual capital. My faith, however, is supposed to be other-centered. That is, it should be directed toward God and my only concern should be whether God is indeed getting a mustard seed's worth of service from me.

That is the reason we are told, "When you have done all you have been commanded to do, say, 'We are useless servants. We have done no more than our duty.'"

Ironically, concern with the depth or breadth of my faith can interfere with my being a slave of duty. I can spend so much time waiting, praying, meditating and contemplating to increase my faith that my mustard seed dries up and dies without bearing any fruit.

Or, I can be ready all the time to respond to the call of God, my master. Even when I think I may have done, I should be ready and willing to do more.

And, more will come. People and situations will always appear that will need a response from this servant of God. The more I respond, the more opportunities for service will open up to me.

An interesting thing will happen as I am busy with this loving service. My mustard seed will sprout and grow without my even noticing it, bearing more mustard seeds that will spread around. So long as I concentrate upon service instead of my mustard seed faith, it will grow bigger than a sycamore.

Twenty-Eighth Sunday of the Year (C)

No matter what the modern diagnosis of the people called lepers in the Gospel might be, their ailment was at least uncomfortable, possibly painful and almost certainly disfiguring (which is how people knew them to be lepers).

As if that were not enough, lepers were considered a source of defilement as well as contagion and therefore were cast off from society, from the religious community and from their families. Many people (and maybe even themselves) thought their affliction was punishment for some evil they had done. They were miserable.

Misery loves company, and it is not choosey about the company it keeps. The ten, being outcasts for the same reason, formed a group. The more interesting thing is that they were able to overcome a different sort of prejudice. They were closed off from the world, but they were open minded. At least one of the group was a Samaritan.

Jews and Samaritans avoided each other. But in this group, Jew and Samaritan came together, stayed together and called on Jesus together. People who normally would have had nothing to do with each other shared life because the rest of the world had rejected them. They were a community.

There are other communities that are formed around a common affliction, a common experience of being different and outcast. Those communities often transcend the prejudices of the society around them, bringing together different races, cultures, social groups and genders. The church is one example.

The church is a group of lepers? Yes, in its essence it is a community of lepers, and to the extent that it is not, it is probably not true to its vocation. That does not mean that we all suffer from skin diseases. What it does mean is that we are disfigured by the sin of the world and by our own participation in that sinfulness.

Since we live in a world of people marred by sin, perhaps we don't notice the extent of our own marring. If we did, our parishes might be more like communities. If I realized how outcast I am from real life in Christ, I might be more open to others and more forgiving of them. My life would have room for the "Samaritans."

And those people whom I would ignore unless I accept how alike we are might teach me something. The Samaritan in the Gospel realized something the rest of his community did not. He realized that when all is said and done, the community's focus must not be upon itself and its needs, but upon Christ.

Jesus sent the lepers to the priests to be verified as clean and offer a sacrifice. On the way, they were healed. That undoubtedly made them joyful and grateful. So, they continued on their way to the temple, following Jesus' instructions.

The Samaritan would not have been with the others. The temple of the Jews was in Jerusalem; that of the Samaritans was at Mt. Gerizim. So, they were going in different directions. The Samaritan was not with the crowd, and there was no reason to go along with what the crowd did. Someone who is "different" can see things the rest of us miss. (Incidentally, that is why the men who run the church must listen to women, the rich must listen to the poor, governments must listen to minorities, adults must listen to children etc.)

So, the Samaritan disobeyed and headed back to say "Thank you." He or she realized that the healing symbolized a relationship with Jesus that was more important than the cure. Verifying the cure was less important than doing what was right in that relationship, saying thanks.

We receive many gifts from God, but it is not the gifts nor even the recipient, but the Giver, upon whom we should focus. For Catholic Christians, the Eucharist is the "source and summit of the Christian life," and *Eucharist* literally means "thanksgiving."

We should be thankful to the ten lepers who teach us to be church. Individually and as a body, we are not true to the image of God. If we can admit that, we can rely upon each other and serve each other in humility. We will exclude no one. We will be a community. That is what the group teaches us. One among that group goes further, and teaches us that our community must be alert to the gifts of God and grateful for them, a gratitude expressed in, above all, the chief prayer of thanksgiving, the Eucharist.

Twenty-Ninth Sunday of the Year (C)

The story of the unjust judge is supposed to teach "the necessity of praying always and not losing heart." It does not achieve that very well for me, because of the image it presents of God, an unjust judge. So, let's ignore Jesus' purpose for a while and look at the parable from another perspective.

The judge's decision is forced by something the woman does that seems natural but is very precious, speaking out. She was able to go to the judge again and again to call upon him for her rights. It is easy to imagine her accosting him on the street and telling him off in front of his friends. She may have stood outside his home, shouting at him to decide her case. The judge was not worn down simply by whispered conversations or politely worded notes. The widow made his life miserable. He even feared that "she will end by doing me violence."

The widow's persistence earned the recognition of her rights. But, what if, like so many people in her day and ours, she had not been able to speak out? What if saying anything against a judge would have cost her liberty or life? It was her freedom to speak that made her able to force the judge to act. Her freedom of speech freed the judge.

Freed the judge? Until the judge acted, he was unjust. The woman was right to expect him to do his job and as long as he failed to do it, he was betraying his position and depriving society of the benefits of his work. The widow forced him to perform his duty. She did not turn him into a good man; he remained one who cared "little for God or man," but at least he had done his job.

Those in power who fear what people — especially those who have been deprived — have to say deprive themselves of the opportunity to change their lives for the better — in other words, of the chance to repent.

This is not true merely in the political realm. The church contains not a few leaders who prefer to not hear voices that call for greater faithfulness to the Gospel. Ultimately, they deprive themselves and the church of the chance to improve.

The widow's persistence is the only answer. Speaking out for the right to those who do not want to hear, whether in society, the Church, our homes or wherever else, is the only cure.

Doing that takes courage and commitment. The widow had to be willing to face the judge, to shout in the streets, to become a pest. Her willingness brought what she was after, action by the judge.

Where can we find that sort of courage and commitment? Perhaps it is time to bring these reflections back to the issue that Jesus was talking about when he taught this parable, prayer.

There are many things that go on when we pray. We petition, we thank, we repent, we adore. More memorably put, the four kinds of prayer are "please," "thanks," "oops!" and "wow!" It is in regard to our prayers of petition, our requests to God, that Jesus tells us of "the necessity of praying always and not losing heart."

Prayers of petition make little sense intellectually. After all, God knows what we need without our asking. Yet, prayers of petition are the kind Jesus recommends most, and the Lord's Prayer itself is one of them. So, we should continue to offer them, regardless of our intellectual doubts.

Whatever else may be a result of prayers that tell God what to do (even if phrased so as to let us think we are making humble requests), we get experience in turning to the powerful and making our desires heard. We all have total freedom of speech when speaking to God. We can turn to God and demand, "Give me justice!"

Perhaps our prayers of petition are, among other things, practice in finding the courage to speak. If we can do it with God, perhaps we can become more able to speak out with people, including the person we see in the mirror, saying, "Give me justice!"

The model in today's Gospel is not God as the judge but the widow as us. We should pray, but our prayer should be practice for speaking out in the world to the unjust judges, the powerful who need to hear the call to justice.

Thirtieth Sunday of the Year (C)

We are living in the very early days of a phenomenon that will reshape Christianity. It has been called "the coming of the Third Church," a phrase based upon the history of Christianity. The First Church, that of the early followers of Christ in the Eastern Mediterranean area, became the Second Church, one centered in Europe.

The Third Church has no center, because it is worldwide. For many in the Catholic Church, the first sign of the coming of this Church was the Second Vatican Council, when photos of the world's bishops showed, for the first time ever, large numbers of African, Asian, Latin American faces and ones from the Pacific. In the half century since, the phenomenon has grown.

What is distinctive about this church? Just as Christianity in the West has been deeply influenced by the religious traditions and cultures that pre-dated the preaching of the Gospel in Europe, so, too, are the Churches of Africa, Asia, Latin America and the Pacific shaped by the religions and cultures that preachers of the Gospel encountered there.

That means that ideas of God, of holiness, of worship, of community, of ministry — of everything that makes a church — are gradually becoming different from what has been "normal" for more than a millennium and a half. Cherished and time-honored traditions and formulations of faith are being called into question.

This is where the parable of the Pharisee and the tax collector has something to teach us. The Pharisee says, "I give you thanks, OGod, that I am not like the rest of men." He goes on to say how he obeys all the rules that have been handed on to him. His boast is that he does what everyone everywhere has always felt should be done.

And he is right. Jesus does not accuse him of lying. He is a good man — he is, after all, trying to pray, and pray with gratitude to God. His problem is that he thinks his own way of appearing before God is the only way. He cannot conceive of someone like the tax collector having a valid relationship with God, even though the tax collector is in the same temple, engaged in the same activity, prayer.

The tax collector, on the other hand, seems barely a member of the People of God. His way of life makes him an outsider. He knows he is different, yet feels that he, too, has some right to be in the temple, praying as best he can.

The tax collector is an apt symbol of those churches that are not only trying to find ways to believe within their own contexts, but will over time change the way all Christians believe.

Since Christians of the Third Church, especially in Asia, are often a powerless minority in their societies, they tend to view the role of the Church and its institutional forms from a different perspective from that of the West, where the Church is only now beginning to face the loss of political, moral, social and intellectual power.

As a religious minority, these Christians are faced with questions that Western Christians have not faced in centuries, if ever. As they struggle to find answers to new questions, some of those answers will appear inadequate to those who faced and answered different questions. Some will actually be inadequate, as inadequate as Western theological formulas and practices. Our theology of the Trinity, for example, may take now-unforeseen directions as Christians in largely Hindu India try to explain what we believe about God.

On various levels, the churches of the West (which are still in charge) have had mixed reactions to the coming of the Third Church. Sometimes, there is rejoicing that the Holy Spirit is working in new ways in new places. Sometimes, there is fear of the unknown and a refusal to allow others to make their own mistakes as the West made and makes its own. Many times, the phenomenon is ignored.

Love it or fear it, a new church is being born. It will take several lifetimes, but eventually the church throughout the world will be different because of what is happening at the back of the temple. The future is there. It would be a shame to miss one of the biggest events in the history of Christianity because like the Pharisee we thought the way we are is the way to be.

Thirty-First Sunday of the Year (C)

Catholics do penance after confession. Penances usually take the form of prayer, but sometimes almsgiving, fasting, restitution or some activity to "let the punishment fit the crime" are recommended by the confessor.

Originally, what we know as the sacrament of penance was performed publicly, and in some places only once in a lifetime. It was only used in the case of major sins that harmed the life of the community — adultery, apostasy and murder.

However, in Ireland and Wales in the fifth and sixth centuries, the practice arose of people meeting with someone to discuss their life as Christians. Manuals called "penitentials" were compiled for these guides. The penitentials list sins and the appropriate penances for each. This practice spread and eventually evolved into the way we celebrate penance today.

Why do penance in the first place? Since penance follows absolution, it cannot be that we are buying God's forgiveness. Christ has already won our salvation. It is not for sale.

Zacchaeus was not looking for salvation. He was "trying to see what Jesus was like." Eventually he climbed a tree to get a glimpse. He got more than he expected.

Jesus answered Zacchaeus' curiosity by inviting himself to dinner. To eat with someone means to accept that person. Zacchaeus was a traitor, collecting taxes for the conquerors, and tax collectors became wealthy through grabbing all they could get over and above the actual high taxes. Yet Jesus says that Zacchaeus is accepted by God. No wonder the crowd started grumbling.

Zacchaeus was not the type to back down, however. He hadn't let the crowd keep him from seeing Jesus. His career was built on not caring about what others thought. So, he "stood his ground" and spoke out.

He announced the penance he was willing to undergo in response to Jesus' forgiveness. It would mark the beginning of a new way of living. He would give half his possessions to the poor and repay fourfold anyone he had defrauded.

Jesus' response was, "today salvation has come to this house." Every member of Zacchaeus' household — his family, his servants and probably even his dog — had suffered because of his sinful life. Now, they would all be beneficiaries of his being forgiven. God's love was wide enough to include them all.

Like Zacchaeus, I am a sinner. Like Zacchaeus, I am loved by God. Like Zacchaeus, I am forgiven, a forgiveness I celebrate most explicitly in the sacrament of Penance.

Like Zacchaeus, I have caused damage that cannot be revoked. The world is marred by my sin. God will use that marring in building the Kingdom, but it is a marring nonetheless.

Healing is needed, just as repaying the defrauded taxpayers was. Penance is an attempt to aid that healing.

Conversion is needed. I must live freed from the power of sin. Penance is a first step in that new life.

Apology is needed. My sins have hurt others in ways I or even they might not realize. Penance is a way of apologizing.

Awe is needed. I should realize the weight of my sins and the even greater weight of God's forgiveness. Penance, which is usually somehow proportional to my sin, is a measure of the great love of God.

Thanksgiving is needed. Forgiveness is a gift. The Lord looks at me as he did at Zacchaeus and says, "I want to be with you." Penance is thanks for that gift.

We usually think of penances as something we do in connection with confession. However, in addition to priest-given penances, I should sometimes impose penances upon myself. I know my sins better than a priest does, and I probably know the appropriate ways to do penance for them.

It is important, though, to remember that penance is neither punishment nor the purchase price for forgiveness. So it should not be extreme. When in doubt, don't do it or consult with someone first.

And what forms should penance take? I can volunteer to help at a soup kitchen, or tutor a child or visit a shut-in. I can make contributions to individuals or organizations that need help. I can work at being a cheerful, cheering presence at home and in society. I can pray for those who have been touched by my sin. I can fix what I have broken. I can fast. With the forthright courage of Zacchaeus, I can proclaim to the world the love of God that "saved a wretch like me."

Thirty-Second Sunday of the Year (C)

A common mistake is to assume that Christianity is about a way of life, a moral system. But before all else, a Christian life is a certain kind of relationship with God through, with and in Jesus Christ. Because we have that relationship, we try to live in a certain way. We know we are loved by God and try to return that love by loving God and all those whom God loves.

One characteristic of that relationship is that it is not ended by death. God's life-giving love is not overwhelmed by my sin will not be overwhelmed by my death.

The Sadducees were not nonbelievers. In some ways they were more strict in their obedience to the Word of God than others, particularly the Pharisees. The Sadducees pointed out that the Torah, the first five books of the Bible, believed to have been revealed by God to Moses, does not mention anything about life beyond death, let alone resurrection.

For most of the history of the People of God between Moses and Jesus, there was no clear belief in an "afterlife." Since the Israelites were surrounded by people like the Egyptians and various Mesopotamian cultures that seemed obsessed with death and its aftermath, this is unusual. Perhaps they had to avoid the issue in order to get their priorities right. The little speculation was vague and certainly did not include resurrection until fairly close to the time of Jesus.

That gives us an important message. Faith is primarily about a relationship with God, not about "getting to heaven" or anything else that smacks of "what's in it for me." Abraham, Sarah, Isaac, Jacob, Moses and the prophets were all people whose faith relied upon God's love for them and their love of God in return, not upon a hope of some form of life beyond death.

The Sadducees who face Jesus are a canny bunch. They use a debating device called the *reductio ad absurdum*, taking their opponent's apparently sensible position and drawing it to a conclusion that shows it to be nonsense right from the start.

They bait Jesus by asking about the case of a woman who married seven brothers. While extreme, it is not absolutely outside the realm of possibility. A widow was expected to marry her brother-in-law if she had not yet borne any children to carry on her husband's line. The Sadducees want to know whose wife she will be in the resurrection, or if she would have a husband for each day of the week. They figured that they had shown how ridiculous belief in resurrection could be.

Jesus refutes them by denying their premise, another debating device. He says they are wrong to presuppose that resurrection is experienced in terms of the life we know. Whatever resurrection means, it is not a rerun.

Jesus goes on to use the Torah to show that resurrection is in line with the ancient faith. The voice that spoke to Moses from the burning bush was that of "the God of Abraham, the God of Isaac and the God of Jacob." But, since God is "God not of the dead, but of the living," then Abraham, Isaac and Jacob are alive.

Jesus affirms the resurrection of the dead, but he does not tell us what resurrection is like. He merely says it will not be like the life we know. There will, for example, be no marriage. But, what will there be? He does not say.

We use lots of images when we talk about resurrection: halos, harps, clouds, a banquet (Jesus himself uses this one). We do that because we need images in order to think, pray and preach about the resurrection. But, we know nothing and it appears we are not supposed to know anything. St. Paul has a rather strong answer for anyone who wonders, "How are the dead raised? With what kind of body do they come?" His abrupt but clear answer: "Fool!" Apparently, we waste time when we speculate upon the resurrection.

All we need know is that God loves us. In that love we live in spite of sin and evil and will live in spite of death. There are no human words or concepts to explain it. All we can confidently say is that it is far beyond what we can imagine or even hope. We're in for a big surprise.

Thirty-Third Sunday of the Year (C)

The people who pointed out the Jerusalem temple to Jesus were overawed. His disciples, after all, were country bumpkins in the big city. They had, perhaps, never seen such magnificence. Since as Jews it was their own temple, they were proud of it and wanted to show it off.

Jesus' prediction in response to their pride, "the days will come when not one stone will be left upon another," was not quite accurate, or at least not yet. Some stones do remain standing on each other, the famous Western or Wailing Wall of the temple mount, a sort of embankment. But, the temple itself is gone without a trace. It was destroyed by a Roman army in the year 70.

Many of the world's great attractions are, like the Parthenon of Athens, ruins. Many things that were once great attractions no longer exist. The same will be true of our modern wonders. The Eiffel Tower, the Great Wall of China, St. Peter's Basilica and all the rest of our constructions will disappear.

Even nature's wonders will wear out, wash out and be gone. The Himalayas and the Grand Canyon will disappear, as their equivalents and greater have disappeared in the past. Even the earth and our solar system have a fairly accurately predicted life span.

Can you name your great-grandmother's great-grandparents? Probably not. They are gone and forgotten. They were born, they lived, they loved and were loved, they achieved and they died. Will your great-grandchild's great-grandchild know your name, let alone your story?

When Jesus talked of a destruction of the temple so absolute that no sign of its having existed would remain, he could have been talking about anything or anybody. He could have been talking about me. As Isaac Watts's hymn *O God Our Help in Ages*

Past puts it: "Time, like an ever-rolling stream,/ Bears all its sons away;/ They fly forgotten, as a dream/ Dies at the opening day."

Is that good news or bad? It certainly is hard to think of it as good news. I know that I must die sooner or later (the later the better). But, to enter oblivion, to have my existence, no matter how significant it appears to me or to others, make no difference to the world is more than I want to think about even though there are some things about my life that I am happy to know will disappear forever.

The thought of our disappearance is so distasteful that we seldom think of it. But, as the church's year draws to an end, we should reflect on the fact that we, too, will draw to an end.

There can be various reactions to our eventual disappearance. The development of cloning techniques has some people thinking that they can somehow be re-created. They forget that cloned people — identical twins — already exist, and they are not the same person. Others live by the ancient dictum, "Eat, drink and be merry, for tomorrow we die," a saying which goes back to the Bible. Since my time here is short, I may as well enjoy it and not worry about what others may think.

There is some truth in that last attitude, but in a sense that might not seem obvious at first. Thought of my death may indeed free me from worrying about what others think — in order to live a life dedicated to God. If I and the scoffers will all be gone one day, why worry about what they may think? Paradoxically, what terrifies some people can give courage to others.

For the one important fact that solely concentrating upon oblivion omits is God. God is not subject to disappearing, and neither is God's love. Those of us who know we are loved by God will disappear, but we are confident that something else awaits us. In the words of the funeral Mass, "for your faithful, Lord, life is changed not ended."

Do I really believe that? Well, sort of. But, there are always doubts. Faith is not certainty, it is a choice. I choose, because of the evidence I have experienced of God's loving help in ages past, to believe that love will not desert me. If I am right, I will know. If I am wrong, I will not know. And in that case, neither being wrong nor having lived at all will matter.

Thirty-Fourth or Last Sunday of the Year
Christt the King (C)

Through much of history, the wealthy and powerful have sat on chairs while the poor sat on stools, benches, overturned buckets or the ground.

The earliest chairs of which we know were made in ancient Egypt. The ancient Greeks and Romans had a kind of portable chair known as a *cathedra*. Since bishops sat on such chairs, the churches that contained them came to be called cathedrals. When the pope declares something to be infallibly the teaching of the Catholic Church, he is said to be speaking *ex cathedra*, from the cathedra. Catholics even speak figuratively of "the throne of Peter" to mean the papacy, though the real Peter may never have sat on a chair in his life.

Chairs still show status. The one who runs a meeting or an organization is called the chairperson. Look in any office, and compare the chairs of the executives with those of their secretaries and receptionists. The higher the position, the bigger and better the chair.

We speak of a bishop's see or the Holy See, "see" coming from a Latin word for a seat. Though priests usually stand to preach, they can, according to the liturgical rules, preach from a chair. Bishops frequently do so. Someone who tells people what to do and how to do it sits.

For a long time, the ruler has been the one who sits. When the ruler stands, no one else may remain seated. This is supposedly the origin of the custom of standing during the Hallelujah Chorus of Handel's oratorio, *Messiah*. When he first heard the music, King George II of Great Britain was supposedly so moved that he stood up. Some claim he was actually bored or had an itch. In any case, everyone else in the audience had to stand as well, and 270 years later audiences around the world continue to do so.

The feast of Christ the King shows another sort of king. This king is not seated; he is hanging on a cross. This king is not wearing fancy clothing; paintings and carvings to the contrary notwithstanding, he is stark naked. This king is not issuing orders; he is under a death sentence.

One more thing about this king — he is ours.

We are followers of a king who has no throne but the cross. What does that mean for us?

A throne-king, a chair-king, is comfortable. The cross-king has forsaken his own comfort for the sake of his people. His people, too, then, should not be concerned primarily with comfort. We should be willing to face inconvenience, discomfort and even death for the sake of others.

A throne-king, a chair-king, has servants and gives orders. The cross-king is humble. His people, too, then, should be servants of all, willing to help all other men and women.

A throne-king, a chair-king, is in his palace, waiting for his subjects to come to him. The cross-king is out where the world can see and hear him, where the world needs him. His people, too, should be in mission to the world, going wherever the Spirit calls them.

A throne-king, a chair-king, condemns. The cross-king forgives and promises a place in paradise to the thief. His people, too, should be forgiving, should be a sign of heaven's love for all.

A throne-king, a chair-king, sits in isolated majesty, surrounded by his courtiers. The cross king hangs between two thieves in front of a crowd of jeerers, soldiers and curious passers-by. His people, too, should be out among the outcasts and sinners, showing them the love of God.

A throne-king, a chair king, is, in spite of all his grandeur, merely one of us. The cross-king is one of us, but much more. He is God with us. His people should be signs of God to the world.

A throne-king, a chair-king, rules geography and the people in it for a few years. The cross-king is the ruler of heaven and of all men and women of all times and climes forever. His people should live as citizens of heaven, not of the world.

We Christians are courtiers of Christ the King, paying him our homage and allegiance. However, we sometimes forget whose subjects we are. We sometimes sit down.

I often become a chair-Christian. I forget where my king is to be found, so I am willing to limit my life of faith to sitting in church, sitting at home, sitting at work, sitting around as the world rushes by.

But, if I am a servant of the cross-king, of a king who does not sit, then I too must not be a sitter. I must show my loyalty to my king by moving among others as he did, as he does, not to receive homage or reward, but to serve.

First Sunday of Lent (C)

I have never gone 40 days without eating. I've never seen the devil in an immediately recognizable form. I cannot turn stones into bread. I've never been offered power over the whole world. I doubt that if I jumped from some pinnacle angels would come to my rescue; I certainly will not try. And yet, I face the same temptations Jesus faced.

"The devil said to him, 'If you are the Son of God, command this stone to become a loaf of bread.'" In other words, the devil tempted Jesus to take care of himself as if even in the face of starvation he were not cared for by God. Not only that, but to look out for himself first by taking the easy way, the quick fix.

I know that temptation. I also know something Jesus did not know. I know about giving in to it. Many times I let my needs and wants become the focus of my attention and action. I think I live by the things of this world, rather than by the ever-present, ever-vigilant love of God. And I am not always careful that the way I meet those needs and wants is in accord with the life I should live as a Christian. I choose to forget that my commitment to Christ is not simply about what I do in church; it is about what I do outside of church. So, rather than trust in God, I act as if God were not part of my life. I look after myself and will do whatever I think necessary to do so.

"Then the devil led him up and showed him in an instant all the kingdoms of the world. And the devil said to him, 'To you I will give their glory and all this authority; for it has been given over to me, and I give it over to anyone I please.'"

Jesus does not contradict the tempter. He does not say that worldly power does not belong to the devil. Nor does he deny that the road to power is devil worship. Instead, he says what the devil offers is not worth the price. Better to be a powerless worshiper of the Lord than a powerful worshiper of evil.

The thirst for power is stronger, perhaps, in the schoolyard, in the workplace or in the family than in politics. Even in the church we often see power at work rather than humble service. And every time we see it, we see a case where the devil has won.

I may not be in a position to rule the world, but there are areas of my own little world where I like to be in charge. I am willing to be a servant, but on my own terms and only as suits my convenience. Otherwise, I will do whatever is necessary to stay in charge, to have some degree of power over myself or others.

"Then the devil took him to Jerusalem, and placed him on the pinnacle of the temple, saying to him, 'If you are the Son of God, throw yourself down from here.'" If Jesus were to do so, the tempter continued, he would force God to rescue him. This is the temptation to make God into a tool.

In my prayer especially, I try to run God, as if God must do certain things because I want them done. Often, those things are good. A mother's prayer for her dying child is certainly no sin. Neither is her anguish and anger when the prayer is not answered as she wished.

The temptation is in the move from "even so, your will and not mine be done" to "my will be done, and you must do it." We must accept the most basic fact of the universe, that God alone is God and the divine will is not ours to control. We live in trust of God's love, confident that whatever else may happen, that love will never desert us.

It is Lent. It is good to begin the season by reflecting upon the temptations that Jesus faced and that we face that hinder us in living the Baptism commitment we renew at Easter.

Easter is God's triumph over sin. It is another point at which we are like Jesus. We are tempted like him, but in our Baptism into his death and resurrection, we are conquerors with him. Jesus faced temptation and refused it. We can be like him in that as well.

Second Sunday of Lent (C)

Is heaven a definite time and place? No. Place and time are within our universe, and heaven is beyond creation. Is heaven, then, totally unconnected with place and time? No. In Christ heaven has come to earth. Is heaven, then, something that was once here, but is here no longer? Is it something that will come?

Those are not idle questions. St. Paul tells us, "As you well know, we have our citizenship in heaven." Someone's this-world citizenship can tell a lot about him or her. If that be so about political citizenship, how much more important is what can be learned from my heavenly citizenship? Curiosity about heaven is not mere speculation. It is an attempt to know who I really am.

Jesus takes three of his followers up a mountain. As he is praying there, he changes somehow. He becomes glorified. What Peter, James and John experienced on that mountain was heaven. It was Jesus in glory, with saints of heaven. We call it "transfiguration." Peter was not sure what to call it, or even what to say.

That is the difficulty with heaven. We do not know what to say. That is not because we are totally inexperienced. The problem is that words just do not suffice. So, we use images. The Gospel uses the image of brightness, of light. We sometimes visualize that by using rays or halos. Sometimes we use the image of freedom that flight symbolizes. So, we put wings on those in heaven. For many, music is the best image of heaven. It cannot be seen, it cannot be touched. Yet it moves us. So, we put harps and horns into our picture of heaven, and we make music an important part of our worship of God who cannot be seen and cannot be touched, but who moves us.

I said we are not totally inexperienced when it comes to heaven. How can that be? Isn't heaven what happens to us, God willing, after we die? Yes. And no. Heaven is yet to come, but it is also present.

I live today as a citizen of heaven, looking forward in hope for full residence in my real homeland. I am on a journey, a life-long journey, toward it. That is heaven yet to come.

Christians have been criticized for being so concentrated upon heaven as a goal that we ignore the world through which we journey. Though there may be some Christians who live that way, the criticism is not fair. The real Christian life is indeed in heaven, but it does not begin when life in this world ends. Heavenly life begins with the death we call Baptism. Heaven is all around me today.

Heaven was present to Peter, James and John on the mountain. Where Jesus is, there is heaven. So, if I wish to experience heaven, I should come to know Jesus better. That means growing in friendship with the Word of God in Scripture. It means prayer.

Another experience of heaven, one that is hard to believe, perhaps, but which is true nonetheless, is the church, the People of God. Look around at the people with whom you worship. It is an unlikely looking heaven, no doubt, but those are the chosen People of God, the citizens of heaven. When you are together, you are all experiencing heaven. One day beyond all days, you'll experience the fullness of heaven together.

Finally, we share the Eucharist. Christ unites ourselves to him in the most intimate way. That is the fullest experience of heaven.

Why all this in Lent? Lent is a chance to live our true citizenship. In prayer, fasting and sacrifice, we weaken our ties to the world. We withdraw from our citizenship in this world in order to focus upon our true home, our true citizenship. As we journey toward Easter, we move along in our journey toward heaven.

We spend more time in prayer, in reflection on the Word of God and on Jesus Christ. We gather more often, perhaps, with the People of God for prayer. We share the Eucharist. We spend the season in heaven as we move toward it.

Third Sunday of Lent (C)

The Galileans murdered by Pilate may have gotten off easy in public opinion. After all, Roman rule was not popular. It is easy, though, to imagine the tongue wagging that went on in Jerusalem when the tower at Siloam collapsed. "Well, those 18 must have been big sinners. It was God's punishment, sure enough."

The same sort of talk goes on today. Some people claim to have a clear idea of God's will. They have an advantage, perhaps, because they have discovered that God thinks just as they do. I am certain that God's thoughts are not my thoughts, nor are God's ways my ways. So, I am less certain of what God thinks in specific situations.

I cannot agree that God devises cruel punishments for people so beloved as to be worth the crucifixion of Jesus. If we could be forgiven nailing him to the cross, what sin is beyond forgiveness? Jesus says there is only one, the refusal to accept forgiveness. Not AIDS nor the rain that ruins a picnic nor any other tragedy or mishap, whether big or small, is God's torturing us.

However, I agree on one point with people who are sure they see God's will in the misfortunes that befall others or even themselves. They believe that God is involved in the matter. They are right.

But, what is the nature of that involvement? What could God be doing besides causing the situations from which we suffer?

We are getting ready for our Good Friday commemoration of what God does with suffering. God undergoes it.

The mystery of the cross of Christ is that God suffers. The suffering of Jesus was not deserved — legally, morally and in every way, Jesus was innocent. Jesus suffered because there is something about God's relationship with us that entails the suffering of God.

We feel farthest from God and God seems farthest from us when we suffer. The pain may be physical as in injury or illness, it may be psychological as in depression or rejection, it may be spiritual as when we feel sinful or that God is far off. Whatever the source or sources, we feel that God has abandoned us.

That is, then, when we most feel the need for God. And God is there. Not that God takes the pain away. That is not the message of the cross. Jesus was not removed from the cross until he was dead. He did not rise to new life until he had suffered fully.

God is with us in our pain, doing what anyone who loves us does when we are in pain: God suffers with us. Some religions may talk of the power of God. Christians should proclaim the pain of God, an infinite pain that comes of infinite love.

Much of God's pain (and our own) is caused by us. The things we do to one another, the things we do to ourselves — everything that goes against the will of God breaks God's heart because it goes against our own good. We call it sin.

We are celebrating Lent, the season of repentance. We reflect upon our sinfulness and do what we can with God's help to change our lives. Rather than punishing us, God gives us chance after chance to stop causing divine and human suffering. That is the point of the parable of the fig tree. That does not mean that we can postpone our conversion. Let us not cause God who loves us and whom we love any more pain.

Fourth Sunday of Lent (C)

When we hear "A man had two sons," don't we stop listening? Instead, we think, "Oh, yeah — the Prodigal Son." We think about the son. However, the parable is not about a prodigal son. It is about a prodigal father.

The first thing he does is to give away one third of his possessions, the share that would eventually be inherited by the younger of two sons. Right from the start of the story, then, the one who is "extremely generous, perhaps to the point of wastefulness" – the definition of "prodigal" — is not the son, but the father.

The next thing that happens is that the son leaves home and wastes his fortune. Or, is it? It is time to ask when the forgiving happens in this story.

Can it be when the son faces facts? No, it cannot be then, because no one at home can hear him come to his senses.

Can it be when he turns and begins his journey home? No, it cannot be then because he is too far off for the father to know.

Can it be when he falls at his father's feet? No, it is not then, because the father does not let him finish his confession.

So, when is the son forgiven? The Gospel tells us that the father saw his son while he was still far off. The reason is clear. The father was standing outside looking into the distance for his son's return.

In other words, when the son walked out the door, his father went out, too. He stood there, waiting for his son to come to his senses and return. The father forgave the son's sin as soon as it was committed. All that remained was for the son to come home and accept forgiveness.

So, what follows the son's receiving his portion is not his departure, but the stepping outside of father and son.

That is the point of Jesus' parable. The father, of course, is God, God whose love is so prodigal that no matter what foolishness I commit, forgiveness is there from the start. Jesus is saying that all I need do is come to my senses, turn around and accept the gift God always offers.

The Pharisees and scribes did not like that. They saw Jesus welcome sinners and eat with them. Eating with them was especially offensive. One description of the Reign of God is of a banquet for all God's people. There might, perhaps, be space at the feast for sinners, but that would depend upon repentance and forgiveness at the coming of the messiah.

By welcoming sinners to the table already, Jesus was claiming that God's reign had begun, and that he himself was the host at the banquet. No wonder the Pharisees and religious teachers acted like the elder brother in the parable. They weren't merely jealous of the folks with whom Jesus ate; they felt that the whole meal was premature and presumptuous.

But, Jesus was telling them by what he did and the story he told that God does not wait to forgive us. We are not doomed to remain in our sin until some special time. We don't have to start being good. All we have to be is loved by God, and that is always, whether we know it or not or whether we accept it or not or whether some like it or not.

Lent is a time for me to come to my senses and return to my Father. I do not need fancy words. I do not need to buy forgiveness with good deeds or intentions. All I need is to say, "Father, I have flunked."

Then, we go out to share the Good News that God is waiting for the whole world to come to its senses, waiting to embrace it with the love that is always there for it.

Fifth Sunday of Lent (C)

The scribes and the Pharisees should get credit for honesty. After all, in the case of the woman caught in adultery they could have made believe they were virtuous and started throwing stones. Instead, when Jesus said, "Let anyone among you who is without sin be the first to throw a stone," they "went away, one by one, beginning with the elders."

As we get older, we have more experience of our weakness, so perhaps the oldest realized soonest that they were not sinless. Their honesty and courage in admitting they were little different from the woman gave courage to their juniors to be as honest. So, three cheers for the scribes and Pharisees!

Jesus, on the other hand, is something of a disappointment. There are many things he could have done but did not do. Is doodling in the dirt what we want him to do when a woman's life is in danger? Why didn't he try to rescue her? How did the poor woman feel when he entrusted her fate to a mob of religious fanatics?

Then, after the mob melted away, where was Jesus the teacher? After all, the woman had been caught in serious sin. Was it right to just say, "Run along now, and, by the way, try not to do it again"? Faced with the sin of the woman and the self-righteous violent inclinations of the scribes and Pharisees, Jesus seems rather too nonchalant.

The English Jesuit priest-poet Gerard Manley Hopkins wrote a sonnet that begins,

My own heart let me have more pity on; let
Me live to my sad self hereafter kind.

Hopkins apparently treated his own heart much as the scribes and Pharisees treated the woman — rigorous, demanding and unforgiving. At least some of the time, we all do that. I am my own strictest judge. I look on my sins and refuse to temper my judgement with mercy. Much of my reflection on my life as a

Christian consists of enumerating my faults and then either feeling miserable about them or feeling miserable that I don't feel miserable about them.

But, if we concentrate solely upon our sins (or the sins of others), we are in danger of becoming so self-absorbed that we will be unable to notice, let alone accept the loving, forgiving embrace of God. We must leave room for comfort to put down roots.

After all, it is a season of penitential reflection. I'm supposed to engage in at least some ascetic practice. The season lends itself to concentrating upon my weakness.

Perhaps that is why as we near the end of Lent we take a look at Jesus refusing to get excited about sin. He does not say it is alright to sin. When the crowd pushes the woman forward, he does not deny her sinfulness. His attitude seems to be, "So? She's a sinner. Who isn't? If any of you aren't, then do what you wish with her."

Of course, there was not one of them who was not a sinner. There is not one of us who is not a sinner. That is not, however, the most important thing about us.

Sin is serious, but the most important thing in the world is the love of God that forgives our sins. The scribes and Pharisees had forgotten that.

So, Jesus says that we have to see sin in the proper perspective. He refused to get excited about the woman's sin. Instead, he accepted her sinfulness (and that of the scribes and Pharisees) as a normal part of life. He told her to avoid it, but did not let her sin become the sole description of her existence.

Does that mean that we need not avoid sin? No. I am a child of God. Therefore, there is a certain kind of life that I should live if I am to be true to who I really am. Like the scribes and Pharisees, I should be brave and honest enough to admit that I am a sinner. Then, like the woman going on her way after meeting Jesus, I should get on with my life as a beloved child, a forgiven child, of God.

Passion or Palm Sunday (C)

Though Jesus said that people would recognize his disciples by their love for one another, it is certain that they are more likely to know us by the sign of the cross.

We mark our churches with a cross. We hang it on our walls and around our necks. We even mark ourselves with the sign of the cross as a blessing. We even turn the cross into fancy jewelry.

The cross is so common that we often fail to reflect on what it actually is. We go through the motions of making the sign of the cross without thinking about it.

The Roman way of doing it may have been especially cruel, but in any form, crucifixion is a painful torture. The word "excruciating" ultimately derives from the Latin word for a cross, *crux*. Not only was it an extremely painful way of dying, it was humiliating. Our crucifixes and art show Jesus in a loincloth, but in fact, people were hung up on display stark naked before crowds of people. Dying on a cross was the ultimate in shame. It was repulsive.

Revulsion at the cross was so strong that even a century after the Roman emperor Constantine outlawed crucifixion, Christians apparently still could not bring themselves to depict Jesus on a cross. Possibly the earliest surviving Christian representation of the crucifixion of Jesus (there is a much earlier anti-Christian one) is a carving on a wooden door of the basilica of Santa Sabina in Rome, dating back to about the year 430. It depicts Jesus and the two men crucified with him, but leaves out their crosses. In the background are some buildings with architectural details that merely hint at crosses.

In Holy Week, we reflect upon the cross as what it really is: a horrible torture device. And, we are forced to reflect upon Jesus as abandoned, degraded, tortured and defeated. It is an image that draws a sympathetic response even from nonbelievers.

If the murder of Jesus were all there is to Holy Week, there would still be plenty of matter for reflection. What is it about us humans that makes us able to devise such horrible ways of mistreating one another? Why do we turn to violence in order to deal with those who differ from, challenge or merely annoy us? What can we do to break humankind's addiction to violence?

But, Holy Week calls us to more than just sympathy for the agony of another or guilt feelings over our propensity to violence and cruelty.

For Christians, the cross is, indeed, a horror. But, it is also the means and sign of salvation. So, while shuddering at its ghastliness, we at the same time "glory in the cross of our Lord Jesus Christ in whom is our salvation, life and resurrection."

Holy Week is, more than anything else, a call to what we commemorate on Thursday: Eucharist, another word for thanksgiving.

We give thanks for what Christ has done for our salvation. The New Testament makes it clear that what he went through was something he did willingly, though certainly not cheerfully. He knew that faithfulness to the Father's love and to his own love for us would ultimately lead through his fear, pain, humiliation and death to a deeper experience of that love.

We give thanks to Christ for uniting with us, embracing the fear, pain and death that are an ineradicable part of our lives. At the worst times of my life, Christ crucified is there with me.

We give thanks to Christ for taking upon himself the worst of what we do to one another, entering into our sinfulness and violence. And forgiving it. The worst that we can do, the worst that we have done, has been embraced by God's forgiving love. And so, I can have the courage to turn from sin, knowing that God's love for me is stronger than my sin.

And finally, we give thanks because this Holy Week leads to Easter, the celebration of our baptismal union with Christ in the life-giving love of the Father. Like Jesus, we will die. We will endure our personal way of the cross. And, as for Jesus, that way of the cross will lead us to the fullness of life in God.

Easter Sunday (C)

Today celebrates Sunday at least as much as it does the Resurrection.

Easter is the feast with no date. It is the first Sunday after the first full moon after the vernal equinox. So, it can be any Sunday between March 22 and April 25.

In 1923, the Vatican declared there would be no problem in setting the feast at a particular Sunday every year and 40 years later, the Second Vatican Council repeated that willingness so long as the other Christian Churches agree. So, at some time in the future, Easter may always be, for example, on the first Sunday of April. It does not matter when we celebrate, so long as it is on a Sunday.

The date on which Jesus rose is unknown. The date of the crucifixion on the Jewish calendar was either the 14th or 15th of the month of Nisan, but no one knows for sure how the first-century Jewish calendar matches up with others, and in any case, we don't know the year of the crucifixion. The date was apparently so unimportant that no one bothered to keep track of it.

However, we have never forgotten that Resurrection day was a Sunday, because there is something about Sunday that would not allow it to be forgotten and would not allow the Resurrection to be celebrated on any other day of the week. We even moved the Sabbath from Saturday to Sunday.

What is so special about Sunday? The answer comes in the first of the two creation stories in the Book of Genesis, when God began creating on the first day of the week, Sunday. "God said, 'Let there be light'; and there was light." Sunday is the day of creation, the day of light.

This is where the link between the Resurrection and Sunday comes in. In the Resurrection of Christ, a new creation has begun. "So if anyone is in Christ, there is a new creation: everything old has passed away; see, everything has become new!" (2 Corinthians 5:17). We now see the world and our lives in a new light, the light of Christ that we symbolize by our Easter candle and proclaim in our Easter Vigil liturgy.

Based upon the story of the creation as a week's work, there is another way to view Sunday. It is not only the first day; it is also the eighth day, the start of the first full week for all creation. The work of God has been completed, and now we live with that completed product. Christ is that completion of creation, the first case of creation being all that God's love calls it to be. In our Baptism, we are united with Christ and are "second week" people.

Compared to the proclamation that we live in a new creation and as a new creation, a date on a calendar does not matter. So, we celebrate the beginning of that new life on the feast of creation, the first day and eighth day, Sunday.

Therefore, every Sunday is a special day, a day like no other. That is why we gather to celebrate the Eucharist on this day. We share a foretaste of the banquet that is full union with God and one another in the fulfilment of God's creative will.

Sunday is special for more than being a day off from weekday duties. It is a day outside of usual time. That is the reason people traditionally wear their good clothes on Sunday (reminder of our baptismal robes) and share the best meal of the week (reminder of the heavenly banquet). It should be a day of prayer, but also a day of play and of creativity in union with God who set the lights to play upon the world this day and gave us the joy of the Resurrection.

Every Sunday we re-experience our baptismal union with Christ and his Church. Every Sunday we rejoice that the Lord has risen and has given us a new life. Every Sunday we recommit ourselves to living as a new creation. Every Sunday, we begin a new week of showing to the world what it means to live as children of the light, citizens of the Kingdom of God.

On this Sunday, this Easter Sunday, we remember what every Sunday is because of what happened one Sunday long ago when the mission of the Church was born in the proclamation, "The Lord is risen!"

So, today we say "Happy Easter!" But, we can say as well, "Happy Sunday!"

Second Sunday of Easter (C)

"I'm angry at my mother," said the boy with all the seriousness and solemnity a five-year-old can muster.

"Why is that?" I asked.

He wrinkled his forehead, and pronouncing each word firmly, clearly and slowly, he answered. "She cleaned my room. I didn't want her to clean my room. I didn't ask her to clean my room. She didn't ask me if she could clean my room. She just went in and cleaned it."

"Can you forgive her for cleaning your room?"

"No!" Then, silence. "Maybe." A bit more silence. Then, finally, "Yes — after it's messed up again."

That boy was not different from the rest of us. When I have been hurt or insulted, I am not ready to forgive right away. Sometimes, I never get around to forgiving at all. Usually, if I do forgive, it is because I have received at least an apology and perhaps some restitution.

In other words, I set conditions on my forgiveness. That boy was willing to forgive his mother once his precondition — restoration of the mess — was met. Once my conditions are met, I, too, will consider forgiveness.

That is usual, isn't it? First comes repentance and apology, then forgiveness. However, in the Gospel, the Lord seems to forget part of the process. He does not say, "If you forgive the sins of anyone who repents, they are forgiven." He says, "If you forgive the sins of any, they are forgiven." Apparently, there are no preconditions.

That is what we celebrate at this Easter time, unearned forgiveness. God will forgive us without waiting for us to fulfill preconditions. It's only a week since we recalled how Christ forgave those who crucified him even while they were doing it.

It does not take much reflection to realize that there are many things I have done or failed to do that need forgiveness. I have repented of some of them. For whatever reasons, I refuse or am unable to repent of others. I am unaware of yet others. I am forgiven of them all.

That means that Easter joy is not just about something that happened "once upon a time in a land far, far away." It is about something that has happened to me, still happens to me, and will always happen to me — God's forgiving love.

With all that Easter means, and all that his appearance to the disciples could be, why did Jesus make forgiveness the point of his message? He could have reminisced about the past or told them about death. Instead, he told them to go out and forgive. Why?

The Resurrection of Jesus is the beginning of a new kind of life not only for him, but for his disciples as well. Those who are united with him — and that means all his followers — now share the life of God in a new way. In our Baptism, we are one with the risen Lord; we are the Body of Christ. Because of that, we share the power of God.

When we think of the power of God, we may think of images that provoke awe, or even terror — thunder, lightning, galaxies hurtling through space. But, what God shares with us is not that sort of power. What God shares is the power of God's selfhood, the power to forgive out of love, the power to overcome evil by not letting it limit love.

So, Jesus tell us that the power to forgive is ours. It is the ultimate weapon against evil. That is the reason for not setting conditions, not waiting for evil to somehow weaken before we forgive. We confront it in its strength and overwhelm it with love.

Does that mean that we condone evil, that we look upon the sin of the world (including our own) and say, "That's alright"? No. Such an attitude would not be a confrontation with evil, but a bowing to it. To forgive evil we must first say, "This is evil; it can have no place in God's world; this needs forgiveness in order to be overwhelmed by God's love."

God entrusts us with a great gift. Overcoming evil depends upon our willingness to forgive. It is up to us. We can forgive, or we can refuse to forgive. God will accept our decision. Of course, if we refuse to forgive, refuse to confront sin with the power of

God, we may need some forgiveness ourselves for desertion in the face of God's and our enemy, evil.

Third Sunday of Easter (C)

Just because there are 153 fish flopping around on the beach, don't think the Gospel story is about that particular animal. No, if there are animals in the story of Jesus and Peter at the lake, they are cats and dogs.

Think of a cat entering a room. First, the nose, whiskers and eyes slowly enter. A look to the left. A look to the right. A look up. A look down. A look back. Then, a paw glides in. A look to the left. A look to the right. A look up. A look down. A look back. Then, another paw. A look to the left. A look to the right. A look up. A look down. A look back. It goes on and on.

Now, think of a dog entering, a big dog with a big tail. Thump! Thump! Bound! Bound! Tail wagging, drool dripping, tongue lolling. Furniture bumped, tabletops tail-swept.

People have a lot in common with cats and dogs. Perhaps that is why they are our favorite pets. There are cat people who like to plan things out. I am one of them, though I prefer dogs. We check out the possibilities and options before carefully committing ourselves. We are also the ones who frequently have to clean up the mess left by dog people.

Dog people rush in, not giving much thought to consequences. They think that problems need not be headed off, since if they happen they can be fixed later, usually by cat people.

Peter was a dog person. Who else when surrounded in the Garden of Gethsemane would pull out a sword and try fighting a gang of professional swordsmen? Who else would *put on* his clothes to jump in a lake for a 100-meter swim?

The others in the boat, cat people for sure, realized that rowing would be more efficient than swimming, so they rowed ashore. "One, two, three, stroke! One, two, three, stroke!" Peter just jumped overboard. If he had possessed a tail, he probably would have swamped the boat with its wagging.

Throughout the Gospels, Peter is always jumping into things. Often, he goes wrong. If he had that tail, it would often be between his legs. Peter has the distinction of being the biggest jerk in the New Testament. And yet, the Lord chose him to be the leader.

In day-to-day life, I prefer dealing with other cat people. We are careful and canny. Dog people exasperate us. However, when it comes to my life of faith, I wish I were a dog like Peter.

John's Gospel talks of the disciple whom Jesus loved. But, when today Jesus asks Peter, "Do you love me more than these?" The answer is an immediate doggy "Yes!" Peter doesn't think about consequences, Peter doesn't plan, Peter doesn't prepare a way out because Peter has only one thing in his mind and heart — his love for Jesus. Peter may not have been "the disciple Jesus loved," but he was the disciple who loved Jesus most.

I wish I could love the Lord in that way — no calculation, no holding back, no double-guessing, no doubts.

Can a cat become a dog? No, but I think and hope cat people can become dog people. It is not easy. Compared to it, bioengineering is child's play. How can it happen?

It takes effort on our part. We have to grow in love of the Lord to the point where we one day find we are getting doggy. The first step is prayer. We must come to know the Lord as one who loves us as a dog. (After all, going to the cross is a dog person's act.) Reflection on our experience and upon the Word of God will deepen our awareness of Christ's love. Gathering with our fellow Christians to share the sacraments, especially the Eucharist, is essential. Perhaps most important is to imitate the Lord's dog-like love. We must begin to lay aside our calculations and considerations and start loving others in deed as well as in speculation.

When we do that, we will see the love of God working through us. We will know that God's love is surrounding us, using us. And we will begin to find the courage to love in return.

Peter was chosen to lead the disciples, to lead the church, not because he was bright or well-spoken or a deep thinker. He was appointed to look after the Lord's flock because he loved the Lord.

Heaven is full of dog-people. The place is probably a messy chaos, with no order, no calm. Just lots of song and dance (the human equivalent of yelping tail-wagging) because of the joy of those who are with the one they love.

I sometimes fear that even if cunning, calculating, considering, careful cats get there, we will miss half the fun.

Fourth Sunday of Easter (C)

We often make the mistake of thinking that being a Christian means living in a certain way, doing certain things. Simply put, it means "being nice." At times, it may mean being extraordinarily "nice" or even heroically "nice." In any case, we think it means obeying certain rules, particularly one that says we should love our neighbors.

That is certainly part of our Christian life, but it is not the core of that life. Living a certain kind of life that involves doing good for our neighbor must be a result of our faith, but is not the faith itself. The core of our faith is in a short passage — only four verses — from the Gospel of John that is this Sunday's reading.

Faith is, first and foremost, a response to a call from the Lord. We are his sheep who hear his voice. And that voice is not some generalized invitation, a "Hey, guys, come with me." The Lord addresses each of us individually, inviting us one by one to follow him. That is what he means when he says he knows his sheep. Sheep may all look alike to the unpracticed, uncaring eye; however, the shepherd can tell them apart.

The two billion or so Christians in the world also look generally alike. There are, of course, variations of gender, build or race, but to some hypothetical visitor from outer space who did not love us, we would probably seem pretty much the same.

But Jesus is not some unloving visitor from outer space. He loves us. So, he calls and cares for us one by one. He knows who I am and calls me by name.

What he calls me to is eternal life. For whatever reasons of his own, in his love Christ has called me to be one who "shall never perish." Or, more accurately — since that infinite love is given to all people — he calls me to know that gift and the love that gives it.

I have seen enough corpses of Christians (and expect to be one myself some day) to know that whatever this promise of eternal, imperishable life means, it does not mean an escape from death. Christ died in order to rise. I, too, must die in order to fully experience the eternal life to which he calls me.

Jesus gives us reason to be hopeful in the face of death. "No one shall snatch them out of my hand....there is no snatching out of the Father's hand." Jesus affirms his identity with the Father in the context of a guarantee. Death shall certainly take us, but it can never snatch us away from the loving care of God, the life-giving love of God. So, we will live as long as that love lives — eternally.

What then of my day-to-day life? Should I just drift along, every so often (an hour each Sunday, for example) remembering that I have been promised eternal life, but otherwise being indistinguishable from my neighbors who do not know that promise?

If I do so, it is a sign that I probably do not really believe what the Lord says. It is, after all, hard for anyone after adolescence to really believe that he or she is going to live forever. I mouth the Creed, saying I believe in "life everlasting," but that declaration does not shape my life.

A Christian is not basically someone who does nice things. A Christian is someone who has been chosen to know God's promise of eternal life. Knowing it, really knowing it in the depths of my being, means that I will live a particular sort of life.

I will not fear the tongues or opinions or other weapons of the world, because I know that they are nothing compared to the eternity I am living. I can take the risk of loving other people, sacrificing my time, talents and treasure in their service because I know I have all eternity.

I do good not because that is what makes me a Christian, but because what makes me a Christian — the promise of eternal life — frees me to do good.

It is still Easter time. It is still the season of the Resurrection. It is still the season to recall that my life is not a matter of the merely day-to-day, but of eternity.

Fifth Sunday of Easter (C)

Jesus says, "This is how all will know you for my disciples: your love for one another."

Our record of loving one another is not good. In the fourth century, we started killing one another for holding different theological opinions. We've stopped the physical torture and killing, but the Vatican office that ran the Inquisition still exists (with a name change) and its methods still shock those who see it in action against fellow Christians.

Saint Robert Bellarmine was instrumental in having the philosopher Giordano Bruno burned alive in part for saying that there might be life on other planets and in getting Galileo imprisoned. *Saint* Joan of Arc led troops who ravaged the countryside when not killing fellow Catholics for the sake of the Kingdom of Charles VII, not the Kingdom of God. Then, her Catholic rivals burned her alive.

The wars between Catholics and Protestants in 16th century Europe were among the most vicious in history. In Ireland, Lebanon, Croatia, Serbia and many other places, we've killed one another using the name of Christian communities — Catholic, Orthodox, Protestant — as our labels and war cries. A poster I saw rightly says that a major step toward world peace would be for Christians to stop killing one another.

In the past century, we experienced two world wars, both occurring in large measure in the so-called Christian part of the world. The wars fought elsewhere and the other violence perpetrated around the globe today use weapons and techniques developed in what is left of "Christendom."

Majority Christian societies are no more loving than other societies. Even in nations dotted with churches we find lies, cruelty, injustice, racism, oppression and the treatment of men, women and children as economic, social, sexual or political tools.

Our Christian homes are no less prone to violence, coldness and hatred than those of any other families. My own Christian heart cannot show the world the unadulterated love of God.

Our love for one another? It's little wonder that after two thousand years we have not converted the world to Christ. The problem is not with the world's vision. The problem is with us. We Christians have not even converted ourselves to Christ.

The place to begin looking for an answer is in the case I know best, my own. Why do I not love as I know I should, as I know I could?

The problem is that the love of God has too small a place in my belief. I find it hard to really believe deep-down that the creation and sanctification of the world is done out of love for me. I don't think I'm worth that kind of love, and I am not. No one is, but God gives it anyway.

Because I find it hard to believe that God can love me, I fail to make love the source of all my life and action.

The Cross and Resurrection of Jesus mean many things, but one of the chief messages of our redemption is that God's love for us is unbounded, uninhibited. We can sin, and God loves us. We can run away, and God loves us. We can spend two thousand years claiming to be disciples with our words while denying it with our deeds, and God loves us. We can die, and God loves us.

For those who are willing and unafraid to see that love (for love, especially that of God, can be frightening), the natural response is grateful love in return. God's overflowing love for me prompts overflowing love in me. I then love — not merely serve — my neighbor. I look like a disciple of Christ.

The task, then, is not to try harder to love my fellow Christians. I must reflect in prayer and stillness upon the love God really has for me. I should be constantly alert to see God's love at work in the events and people around me.

If I can believe in that love, then the world may see a new kind of Christian, a new kind of church, one that lives as Jesus did, as Jesus does. When that happens, the world will know that I, that we, are companions of Jesus. The world will experience that love, be drawn by that love, and join in that love.

Bringing the world to Christ is our vocation. Loving one another is the way to live that vocation.

Sixth Sunday of Easter (C)

Throughout the history of God's relationship with us, there are many cases of people disappearing just when you would expect they would get some well-earned rest and glory. Moses leads the Hebrews out of Egypt and through the desert for 40 years to the edge of the Promised Land, but then dies without entering it. There are men and women in the Old Testament whose sole reason for appearing seems to be to ensure that there is a next generation.

Even in the New Testament, people disappear. Once Jesus is found by his parents in the Jerusalem Temple as a boy, Joseph disappears from the story. In the first chapter of The Acts of the Apostles, Luke mentions that Mary was among the women who gathered with the disciples following the resurrection. That is the last we hear of her in Scripture.

In John's Gospel, Jesus prepares his disciples for his own departure after his death and resurrection: "I go away for a while, and I come back to you."

God seems to work on the principle that people are to serve a function, then move on. We call it "vocation." Catholics often assume that "vocation" refers solely to a call to the ordained or consecrated life. It is actually a call to spend a lifetime trying to live faithful to our growing understanding of what God hopes for us. That may mean ordination or vows, but they are not, in most cases, the way to live one's vocation.

In the Bible, men and women who have fulfilled their vocations have no more reason to stick around. Their task is done and they move off the stage. So, is the sopping paper towel the symbol of our lives? Used, used up, and tossed away when we no longer serve a purpose? Is the goal of our lives God's wastebasket?

The going away of Jesus proves that we are not bound to be God's trash. Jesus says that his going is not only linked to God's chief gifts to the disciples, but that his going is a necessary prerequisite to that giving.

There are two gifts that are linked to Jesus' leaving his disciples — peace and the Holy Spirit.

"Peace is my farewell to you," he says. In one sense, this is a trite statement. "Peace — *shalom*," was the normal greeting and farewell in Jesus' world. Just as most of us do not intend to say "God be with you" when we say "goodbye," most people who gave "Peace" as their farewell did not think of wishes for peace. It was a conventional greeting.

But Jesus means what he says and confirms that the peace he wishes upon his friends will indeed be theirs: "My peace is my gift to you. I do not give it to you as the world gives peace."

But, that gift of peace is a parting gift. It is when Jesus has fulfilled his vocation and is ready to move on that he can give peace. The man or woman who has found and lived the vocation God gives becomes a peace giver. That may already be true of ourselves at times, if not always.

The quest for peace takes a lifetime. It is not a political peace, nor just an absence of conflict. It is something much deeper. It is union with God, a union that will reach its fullness when we have lived our vocation fully and it is time to accept the reward of our journey.

The second gift of Christ is the Holy Spirit. Jesus fulfills his vocation and becomes a peace-giver. He also gives the means for us to be like him. The gift of the Spirit is essential to growing in our vocation. Without the action of God in us, we could never discern what God calls us to be and do.

The gift of peace would be glorious in itself, but as Christians we have a special vocation. We are called not merely to find peace, but to be the means of peace for others. We must find and live our own vocations, but also be guides and assistants to others in fulfilling their vocation to receive peace.

If by the time our turn has come to move offstage we have been the means of others' finding peace, we will have indeed lived our Christian vocation, served our purpose. We can then joyfully join Moses, Joseph, Mary and Jesus not in God's trash bin, but in God's glory.

Ascension (C)

The Gospel According to Luke and the Acts of the Apostles are two volumes of a single work by the same author. Each volume includes an account of the last encounter of the risen Lord with his disciples before he leaves them.

The first reading in the Mass for the feast of the Ascension is the opening of volume two, the Acts of the Apostles, and tells the familiar story of Jesus parting from his disciples after forty days. The reading from the Gospel are the final words of volume one, and so they immediately precede the words we hear at the beginning of the liturgy of the Word.

But, they contradict each other! Acts has Jesus appearing to the apostles for forty days after his resurrection and then being lifted up. However, the Gospel presents the event as taking place on the evening of Resurrection Sunday in the presence of many disciples and speaks simply of Jesus' parting from them.

If we assume that Luke is reporting facts about the life of Jesus and the Church, there is certainly a problem. Might it be that he had taken a break between writing the two volumes and had forgotten what he wrote in volume one before starting to write volume two? After all, we too have the experience of not paying close enough attention to readings at Mass and missing connections. But how could Luke forget such important facts? On the other hand, and more likely, the differences between the two accounts might give us an insight into how to read Scripture.

One of the mistakes that Biblical fundamentalists make is to assume that when people wrote and thought thousands of years ago, they did so in exactly the same way that we do. They did not. So, a fundamentalist might assume that something is literal reporting when it is actually an ancient writing style that introduces details not for the sake of accuracy, but as spurs to memory or thought.

So, unless we want to say that Luke did not know what he was doing as he moved from writing the Gospel to writing Acts, we must admit that some of his "information" that we reflect upon today is meant to tell us truth rather than facts.

There is a difference between truth and fact. Something can be truthful without being factual. For example, the two accounts of creation in the book of Genesis tell us the truth that God creates and considers the world something good. It assures us that our existence is not absolutely divorced from the concern of God. However, if we want the facts about the universe, we must go to scientists.

On the other hand, something can be factual without being true. If truth be what is in accord with the will of God, then sin, injustice and violence are not true, merely factual. And, since we follow Christ who is the Truth, we confront, repudiate and combat such facts for the sake of truth.

So, if we admit that Luke is not trying to present facts in his different accounts, what is the truth he hopes to convey to us?

The Gospel account, by having Jesus ascend to glory as an immediate part of his Resurrection, stresses that the glorification of Jesus is an effect and part of the Resurrection, not something separate from it, an add-on. And, by having all the disciples there, men and women, Luke is affirming the missionary vocation of all the followers of Jesus.

In the Acts of the Apostles, Luke's placing the Ascension 40 days after the Resurrection brings to mind the 40 years that the Hebrews wandered in the desert on the way to the promised land. In Scripture, 40 days, weeks or years are not exact measures of time, as if we can assume that there were 960 hours between the Resurrection and the Ascension. The number means a long time, long enough for people to become what God intends them to be.

And that is part of the truth that opens the Acts of the Apostles, the volume of Luke's work that presents the new community, the new people of God, going out into the world to proclaim the Good News. They are now ready to take up the mission of the Lord.

Acts tells a truth about us. We, the new people of God, have been prepared for our vocation. We are the apostles. Christ has stepped aside so that we might step forward. The Acts of the Apostles begins with the Ascension of Jesus; they continue with us.

Seventh Sunday of Easter (C)

If John's community were living in harmony, there would have been no need to waste ink calling for it. By including Jesus' prayer "that all may be one," John is telling friends and foes in his community, "Hey, gang, let's try to do what the Lord wants of us."

Right from the start, followers of Christ have not been united. The epistles of St. Paul, the earliest writings in the New Testament, show that we have been contentious, pig-headed and fractured into factions right from the start.

There are obvious divisions in the church. We talk of Anglicans, Catholics, Orthodox and Protestants. There are others who would be welcome in none of those groups. Even within these groups, there are divisions based upon politics, history, language, theology, selfishness and plain stupidity. We back-bite, bicker and sometimes even kill one another over our ways of following Christ. The ecumenical movement uses Jesus' prayer as its mandate and motto with good reason.

Though scholars point to hints in the Gospel of John of divisions between his community and others (particularly that which followed Peter), he was probably not thinking solely of divisions between communities when he decided to include Jesus' prayer for unity in his Gospel.

If the only divisions among Christians were among churches, it would still be a scandal, but on the level that really matters — the lives of individual Christians — it would not necessarily hamper union in prayer, reflection and action.

The real problem is that even in our local communities we do not have unity. Anyone who has endured a meeting in any congregation knows that. One need not even go to a meeting to see it. Go to a church that has a parking lot, and as you watch the jockeying for spaces or the rush to the exit, you can see whether or not Christians are united in love as brothers and sisters. It's not a pretty sight.

Our lives outside the church grounds are no better signs that Jesus' prayer for unity has been fulfilled. In our day-to-day lives, we seldom, if ever, give thought to the fact that someone with whom we are dealing is a fellow Christian. If the thought crosses my mind, I decide it is irrelevant to the matter at hand. That matter may, in fact, be something I am doing to that fellow Christian that I eventually may have to confess as sin.

Obvious divisions are not, however, the worst sign that the prayer of Jesus has not been answered and that we have been the ones who have blocked the answer. Far worse than active divisions, rivalries and conflicts is plain indifference.

Jesus does not pray that we not be divided. He wants something positive, some quality of life and action called unity.

When I look at the average Christian community, I do not see division so much as I see indifference. We can sit next to one another on a Sunday, proclaiming one faith, hearing the one Word of God, partaking of the one Eucharist and sharing eternal life with one another, and yet not bother to say "Good morning." We do not know each other, and too often do not care to. We cannot welcome newcomers because we probably do not know the old-timers well enough to recognize who might be new. We are not divided, but we are certainly not united, not one in the love of Christ.

There are, of course, excuses for this. Many of our parishes are too big; too many of our leaders do not foster unity; modern society hinders our ability to form community. All of this can be true, but the fact remains that the Lord has prayed for unity, and no excuse should block that prayer's coming true.

What shall we do? Until we refuse to be satisfied with mere lack of division, and become dissatisfied with lack of unity, Jesus' prayer will be thwarted in our lives.

For the sake of unity, some divisiveness may be necessary. I may have to care enough to complain, to make demands. I may have to engage in activities that foster unity in our communities. I may have to become unpopular with those who are comfortable avoiding the demands of community or who fear the unknown. I may have to overcome my own reluctance to be truly one with anyone whom Jesus has made one with him and me in Baptism.

It is a big challenge. But, it is also a chance for me to answer Jesus' prayer, a nice way to offer thanks for the prayers God has heard from me.

Pentecost (C)

"Peace be with you," was the greeting the risen Lord gave his fearful disciples. "At the sight of the Lord the disciples rejoiced." The first gift of the Kingdom is joy-giving peace and Pentecost is a feast of that peace.

The same spirit that swept over the waters at creation came over the disciples to make a new creation: "From heaven there came a sound like the rush of a violent wind ... All of them were filled with the Holy Spirit."

The next thing that happened was the birth of the church in mission. The disciples who had been hiding in fear now praised God for all the world to hear. Peter, who had once denied even knowing Jesus, stood before a crowd and proclaimed that Jesus was risen. According to the Acts of the Apostles, three thousand people who heard him were baptized. This new creation meant to include those of "every race and tongue, every people and nation."

So, today's feast is a celebration of our mission as Church to proclaim to the whole world that Christ is risen. Since it is also a day on which we recall Christ's gift of forgiveness, we must reflect upon the sins that might hinder that proclamation.

There are, of course, many circumstances where hindrances to our proclamation come from outside ourselves. There are places in the world where Christians are forbidden to share the good news of the Resurrection.

However, probably the biggest obstacle to people's accepting the Gospel is we Christians. Our sin keeps people from hearing and accepting the call of God to know Christ. Today, we are challenged to examine ourselves for a terrible sin against creation and to recommit ourselves to fighting it.

When the new creation began, "the crowd gathered and was bewildered, because each one heard them speaking in the native language of each." Parthians, Medes, Elamites, Mesopotamians,

Judeans, Cappadocians, Pontians, Asians, Phrygians, Pamphilians, Egyptians, Libyans, Romans, Cretans and Arabs — a lector's nightmare of hard-to-read names — were able to hear the Good News.

The Kingdom of God makes no distinctions. All hear the proclamation "about the marvels God has accomplished." The Kingdom of God, the new creation, has room for all. Yet, we make many distinctions in our personal and social lives, distinctions that betray what God has done. God created the world in variety, yet we refuse to accept God's creation.

The sin has many names because it takes many forms: racism, ethnocentrism, bigotry, prejudice, nationalism, tribalism, genderism, discrimination, snobbishness, intolerance. However, it is basically one sin, the refusal to accept the work of God's spirit in creating the world as the varied place it is.

Sometimes the sin is obvious in its enormity. "Ethnic cleansing" is a new phrase, but not a new reality in our world. The persecution of Jews by Christians throughout history is our indelible shame. Christians have deprived others of their rights and even of life because they were of a different color. We have even killed each other because we have different ways of following Christ.

But, in some ways, the more terrible forms of this sin are harder to see, less stark. There are examples of prejudice in my life that are so much a part of me that I have to make an effort to even notice them.

We hope to spend eternity with men and women who are different from ourselves, but we balk at spending our short lives in this world with them, sharing our societies, our nations, our rights or our goods. Their difference, their God-given variety, is our only reason. All sin is idiotic, and since this sin is a great one it is greatly idiotic.

The people of many backgrounds who heard Peter "were cut to the heart and said, 'What are we to do?'"

Peter's answer was, "Repent." I must admit the sin, see how it manifests itself in my life, and then ask God's forgiveness for denying the creation. I must ask for the courage to confront my sin and not let it control my words or deeds.

That is our hope. Our sins are not unforgivable. God, who by our lights might have reason to discriminate against us, embraces us and offers peace. We who are sent to the world to continue the loving work of the incarnate Son must overcome our unreasoned fear and hatred of others so that we might share with them the joy-giving peace that is the Pentecost promise to all creation.

Trinity Sunday (C)

What does the Trinity look like? Artists often portray the mystery by using images of a white-bearded old man, Jesus and a dove. I don't like those portrayals. The Old Testament very strongly forbids making images of God, a prohibition that Islam also takes seriously. That prohibition makes good sense.

The problem is that what we imagine can become or at least shape what we believe. By turning God the Father into a sort of Santa Claus figure, we are in danger of forgetting the absolute holiness and otherness of God. God the Father can become more like an indulgent uncle or a stern grandfather. In other words, we are in danger of making God in our image instead of recalling that it is the other way around. God has made us in the divine image.

However, for Christians, there is one exception to the rule, an exception that God has made. If we wish to portray God, we must portray Jesus, God's self-presentation in material form. In the Incarnation, God has said, "If you want to know what I am like, look at me in Jesus."

Of course, the New Testament does not tell us what Jesus looked like, and so we use our imagination to visualize him. Since until recently most Christian art has come from the West, many artistic portrayals of Jesus make him look like a European, though he was not one. Increasingly, artists now show him with Asian, African or other features.

But, more important than his looks is what Jesus did and does. We must look to his words and deeds if we want to know about God, want to know God. And his foremost deed and the clearest picture of the Trinity is the Cross.

The Cross is not merely something that happened to Jesus long ago. On the Cross, we see absolute love in action. That love is a self-giving that holds nothing back. Jesus offered himself to the Father totally on the Cross. That is the heart of the mystery of the

Trinity, an absolutely unlimited self-giving love among the Father, Son and Holy Spirit. On the Cross, God the Son shows what absolute self-giving looks like when it is enfleshed. It is a handing over of one's life, and through that a receiving of new life.

Scripture tells us that we are created in the image of God. In that case, there must be something about the mystery of the Trinity that tells us about the mystery of ourselves. Who am I really? Why do I exist? What is my destiny?

Because the unlimited and overflowing love in the Trinity undergirds all of creation, all that exists, including you and I, exists because the Triune God loves us. Because that absolutely self-giving love within the Trinity is the basis of our existence, that means that our own lives find their fullest meaning in self-giving, even to death.

In addition, if we are created in the image of the Triune God, there must be something about us, something about me, that tells something about the mystery of God. Of course, not everything I say or do points to God. My sin, fear, laziness, selfishness and such do not tell me or others about God, except the divine love that shows itself in mercy.

But, when I am at my best, then I do show something about God to the world. When I love, when I forgive, when I serve, when I abandon self-centeredness, then I show the world something about the loving Triune God.

Jesus no longer walks among us to show the world what the Trinity is like. Instead, he has founded a community, the Church, to carry on his vocation of showing God to the world. Today, the most real representation of the Trinity is we Christians ourselves. We are the body of Christ. To know ourselves as we are meant to be, we look to Jesus. To know Jesus as he is, we look to one another, especially to those who suffer on the cross in various ways today.

That is our glory and our shame. Our glory as Christians is that God has chosen us to carry on the mission of the Son to be the love of God incarnate in creation. Our shame is that we so often fail as a Church and as individual Christians to live that mission.

On Trinity Sunday, we know what God looks like. God looks like Jesus. And we know what we must look like. We must look like Jesus.

The Body and Blood of Christ (C)

The Eucharist appears to be an "in-house" affair. We do not share it with those who are not Christians. Except in extraordinary circumstances, Catholics do not share the Eucharist with non-Catholic Christians.

So, the Feast of the Body and Blood of Christ would appear to be a day for a family celebration. But the Mass readings bring gate crashers into our party. The first is Melchizedek, king of Salem and priest of El Shaddai, God Most High. That is all we know about him. He was a pagan foreigner. "God Most High" was some locally worshiped deity of the people of Salem. Since the god belonged to the kingdom and the kingdom to the god, the king naturally served a priestly function.

Melchizedek is probably in the readings because his blessing is connected with bread and wine and the Eucharist is bread and wine. But, whether he is with us for some deep theological reason or merely because of his menu, it is good to have him.

Why? Because of what he does. Melchizedek blesses Abram, ancestor in faith of all who believe in the one true God. But, look at what is happening. There is only one true believer in the world, and he is being blessed by a non-believer in the name of some non-existent tribal god!

God's love and blessings are not limited by the belief of the men and women through whom God chooses to work. A pagan priest-king not only has a place in the building of the Reign of God, but God uses him to bless believers.

Today there are many more believers than in Abram's time. Jews, Christians and Muslims — all of whom worship the same one God — number about three billion. Even so, the people for whom Melchizedek stands still outnumber us. Perhaps they always will.

Because Melchizedek has joined our celebration, all those other billions are part of what we do. They, like we, can be a means for God to bless the world. So, the whole world is with us as we worship, no matter who, what, how or even if they themselves worship. Do you feel a bit crowded?

Luke's Gospel continues this theme of universalism. Jesus tells the disciples to feed everyone. When the disciples are unable to do so, he provides the wherewithal to feed them. Now, everyone there had made some effort to come to Jesus. Perhaps some of them were true believers. Perhaps others were merely curious. Perhaps some went because a friend was going. Whatever their reason for coming, "they all ate until they had enough."

This miracle is about the Eucharist. It is for all who follow Jesus, no matter how mixed their motives. But there is more to it than that. Luke tells us that what they had left "filled twelve baskets." The number twelve symbolizes the whole People of God and so the leftovers show that there is enough even for those who were not there. They were somehow remembered in the action of Jesus. Feeling more crowded?

It is St. Paul, however, who makes the point most strongly. "Every time, then, you eat this bread and drink this cup, you proclaim the death of the Lord until he comes!" We share the Eucharist not for our own sakes, but for the sake of showing the world the saving presence of Jesus among us. What began by looking like a family meal now appears to be a meal the family shares not for its own sake at all, but for the rest of the world!

So, Melchizedek and the mob belong in our thoughts and prayers today. When we share the Eucharist, we do so on behalf of Melchizedek and all others who do not know Christ. God works through them to bless the world, and us with it. We should keep them in mind and heart, giving thanks for them and on behalf of them.

CPSIA information can be obtained
at www.ICGtesting.com
Printed in the USA
FFHW020227081218
49664364-54053FF